Upon Moral Beauty

selected articles by **Eduardo Alexandre Pinto**

We have to learn about dignity

Sat Jun 20, 2015 4:50 pm

A hotbed of a cosmic frontier nurtures its esteem in a plausible scent and beneath the fresh imagination of a certain presence somewhere in the navigation of all Earth kingdoms, it is carried within the doorway into a necessity and that is the pulsation when we complete a circle of perfection: creation from tension to expansion. From the straight vision in us for the Universe we have an unseen respect, a face in articulation, longed in time as justification of the same zeal which launches our dignity. Dignity is a windy spirit with a body promoting the friendly energy which exists in the cosmos, it is one direct whistling as an expanded bowel raised from the fertilization of this conceived talent, we have to learn about dignity.

COSMIC CONSCIOUS

Sat Jun 20, 2015 1:20 pm

There is an endless story in the out space, the awake and the loss of it are inside our cosmic conscious when as humans we feel the cosmos as a natural wonder to feel with respect. Everyone is on the side of it what runs deep, up where the flashing blue light in the Lisbon skies around 1985, where I saw this light for 2 seconds when I was returning home from high school and the relation with the out space had a begin on my life. My view of the cosmos is vast, it crosses speculation, and I only talk and write what I´ve experienced posting the factual virtue following conquers in the relation to the unknown. That is the angelical upstart for any human creature that attends truth from the relation with the cosmos has in everyone's life. It can be a deep feeling coming from the character directed to the front sense of understanding the standing importance of knowing by advance that the mind can be surprised by the visit of every engine of doubt even if it is a blue flash coming from the unknown skies that we know as blue. The fractals combine a multitude of motions, colors call for pleasant amusement as work done, save from the raiders of something unusual and a fortune to hold around our personal story which is involved with the cosmos, it was left to dream about as it is said but it exists.

Heating what is never enough matters the silent hours in which human energy is devoted to think, the self-analysis as good counselor in the interest of the human map in the front line of the first underlined echoes in each note presented as an element of real compassion, moving in own tempo with the equilibrium that you and me can find in the tense logic of the cosmos.

The way to turn the deepness of every feeling inside the movement in far galaxies is related with energy that both generate; the possible interaction with both of the differences is not known but is not time to go to the cosmos to travel or to escape in order to continue the slavery in other sources of life, it should be a relation based on love, then diplomacy which is in pain from what is read, felt, thought, lived in the human conflicts that should take a long breath from the inside to lead the relation with the cosmos with equilibrium and it is one of the reasons of the message of the Sempiternal Pansexuality. The living relation with the cosmos can be a good seed in the outcome of human emergent energy; it must point a sharpened taste for intelligence spoken with the heart, never as fiction but in real level of desire for the sempiternal stability of the Universe.

WORK

Work is energy in movement. Humans caress the outcome of their skills to produce a concrete birth in the maneuvers of hands or by the intellect. To think is work but to be close to nature is seen as a crucified scenario when nothing is visible into the stranger's eyes that is unable to understand the profits of contemplation like children do in wondering about the Universe.

As babies who suck on the mother's nipples, there is pleasure and the mother provides the life source from the organization inside her and out for the benefit of her growing passion together with the cooperation of the man, in due respect for the relation in which the love, knowledge and work are as we might know, the well spring of our lives and we should govern these fundamental resources.

All the stress coming between the working actions provide an inward reflection to push away the hierarchy systems who by force of ignorance but assumed in fashionable artificial ornaments, are in the domain of critics, because the peaceful life is lived in the nature while humans amuse themselves on her but don't take much of her relaxed fragrance to inspire the good melody of harmony. All things are related, relations with humans, nature, the cosmos and it´s up to time the certifying of their philosophical systems if it fits in the peace temper of the life of the semper as it is a hope delivered by the jaded scars in the character so far from the reality which is still lived in some Anarchist Communes and Indian Tribes with a free and healthy example of societies in cities and in the forests.

The discovers where the swimming body goes in relaxed performances, curl the straight lines of the thinking horizon of the seas being the time to be around our ego and hide to seek, the energy that by infatuation is a natural sympathy to the community; it can be as the poets do, philosophers or a man that in broad day light with a lantern warns about all the vertical segments of the need to go back into the land where there is time to observe and act in precise forms of trust.

Trust must be worked for long time in the relations, and then the results are a prolific virtue that satisfies the energy thrown into the others as a new generating motion of solid ground for many generations, fertilized with the conviction of knowing solidarity with justice by emphasis of all effort in the sowing seeds from life´s energies.

Life exists by the lifting on the knots

Mon May 04, 2015 7:15 pm

To be mental in the ideal of a particular color can be a naïf desire with solid ground to proceed by consistence on the existence of a real life in the mind with each difference as long as the challenge does not tear apart from what is known and this is brought to the gender of ideas. The entirely mind and thoughts being clear with the allies of each inner goal that argues for peace and confusion is now empty as nature changes and we combine details with the constitution of perceiving. For example, the images in the actual mental proof on humans that are labeled as having a mental disease where these colors are inside in any doubt being transferred into the faculty act that brings by all exogenous determinisms, many necessary elements in the understanding of what is the mind. To iron little and little the tact that admits the substance in the functionalism for being human with what we can aspire for the reality that is composed by images and words that open a patch that all desires contain a living importance. And as an answer that the hermit had told me: 'it is the fully anticipation in the sense-data of intuition that exists the statement to understand any original reality, therefore to be aware of the domain of what it concerns the good mind in between the human kind'.

Riding home, into the rock cave where the things get softer by the defense of a balneal exposure to the arms into the rocks upon the skin but that doesn't hurt because stones for the hermit, are their natural homeland and a glory for not to shed hope on the way civilization really hurts and puts things away from the natural actions when thought is in control as behavior works wrongly like an empty room without an atom. While the stone has life and that is a small step to understand the difference from matter and existence in all the angles that are in front of our body.

Life exists by the lifting on the knots who proclaim a relaxed start where the things about the hermit were told as they would be told to you dear reader and what is fair in the gist of every scientific approach into the world where the entourage of recreation shows by one side, the dazzling voices and for the other, the anguish population who by bad fortune of the non-self-mastering policies. These people are in serious starvation down in the same ground level where we all live by persuasion of the same existence which life can lift little by little if by the first time, we enter a vast radiant atmosphere, we can enjoy our senses with the energy. By pushing the desire of feelings without the murderous attempt of matter rewards for what is taken here by the cosmic calenture of silence and that means so much more than you and I both know. Maybe that's the fun or the horror of it, we shall see with words and your touch in here, to see what is alive and by swinging in the sunny days and in the hotbed of repose, just like a kind of languor which takes the dog for a walk and we feel part of something. This part is so much more valid if by no fear of the closest unknown around the outside, we can meet new eyes and a face with rising possibilities of going deeper across the conscious of too much awareness.

Holly words of the inner speech

Fri Mar 27, 2015 11:12 pm

Rural spots such as the sexual life of insects, conduct the esteem perusing at the land and mitigating the smooth feeling which answers to the windy spirit known as work. The impetuous alliance upon world citizens conceals emotions in crowd acts but sometimes masses are moving by influence and go with the flow. Rivers know the mystery something in the shape of energy, this fountain of hope obliges all conducts to survey the immanent love as demand of natural needs. There is something near the window where I stood to perceive my garden from a room where my father has put me in to learn about introspection and to prepare my smile upon the holly words of the inner speech, hours and hours as recommendation for adventure. My adventures have taken me into different hours, I among others, we used to dig deeper in dynamic creations often ending in love making or mountain climbing so much before from our rooms where we have had created the provisions for the future. No one has died from it in memory, we were going where the confessions of energy would shine forever but of course the glorious lanes were calm friends of pedestrians like feelings being in motion with the limits of what secures attention. The disposition of my generation intercepted the activity of a deep violet scene, we had white wings and we danced like ink answering shyness, like an eye game played endlessly with selected aspects of generosity into the world.

A secretion of feelings

Fri Mar 13, 2015 10:16 pm

A way to polish eternity as our living signs is to consulate beauty and love within humus embraced with a proper sensibility and disposition of each generation to adopt those of have the soft feathers of the visible energy. The immediate seeker knows how the heart digs deeper in utter thoughts. Me and you, we are the open dialog of bed time, we play, we sing, we believe in what it is painted as routine gathered with work, for the benefit of a growing substance when reason cares for the future and solves doubts by a secretion of feelings.

Majestic Fun

Fri Feb 27, 2015 12:23 pm

The consistence of an accommodation around a clear sky, contents hope and dismantles the movement as decal of the little lane. We all drink from the same fountain as rectors from unknown behavior, finding peace in the settlement of parallels that are found in the daily method to open dialogs in spontaneous manners, often made of repose. Only the love can save the morning after pasting affection with what it stands alike a sermon searching the people who need protection as words mean comprehension into the human best way of the apprehension of all life forms.

The murmur of our life journey

Wed Dec 17, 2014 3:59 pm

To the murmur of our life journey, enhancing the proper spell within the laces which we have, is one vivid reality founded in the virginity of the ages. Humans have to be understood as ambition to oppose and correct the emotional plague among all if possible. Timeless pieces of work have been exposed here and are everywhere, simply because the spirit is one show of strength as a wide-open sky. Again, my Christmas wishes for the Alexander Lowen Foundation with the hope that therapy can reach anyone in this planet, the seeds exist, so to feed them is a capable passage from the devotion time into the realm of the being human, makes of the Foundation a happy place.

A day placed in beatitude

Sat Nov 22, 2014 11:03 pm

Under the corridor, far from the outdoor, sending gifts to the divine being with an open dialog landing in plane love as treasure of a day placed in beatitude.

Bears know parables

Sun Oct 19, 2014 9:27 pm

As a bear knows how to hibernate, grace in them is a parable of wisdom because they make deals with the seasons being themselves in the middle of many of the television skies. Just when we are trying to enter on something leaving us tense and a past in the hands is as important as a future with balance and with the same seasons which I call reason at the calendar to think about.

The perception of Silence

Sun Oct 19, 2014 9:10 am

The perception of silence during the initial solitude portrait while we keep growing with the sowing seeds which are here, in the logic of a zillion stories inside the ear, in every memory sign of a visual sound of the things that are the clamor of understanding by a straight thought which acts with what we hear, feel, wish, dream, in the preparation for silence after it came and keeps coming as we are also our own star dust remedy.

We have to go where the lips are asking

Wed Oct 15, 2014 9:59 pm

We have to go where the lips are asking for kindness, conferring a certain motility on behalf of the world, listening to the silence even if he is not there because a divine being is warm and gentle.

The skills of the media

Wed Oct 15, 2014 9:11 pm

Deepness is affordable when the mind lies on accurate ascensions through levels of thought and reflection, allowing the individual to reach the inner voice with more truly sense than with immediacy. We have to be smarter than the skills of the media.

A singing dream

Wed Jul 30, 2014 2:40 pm

To attend the skills of our natures, we must be under the dream academy of the indigo élan which allows us to perform independence, time after time, just when legacies are passed like all the ideas of the good in this world because a mature universe has no fear neither automatic pain.

Arguing with traffic police may be conclusive

Fri Jul 25, 2014 8:34 pm

Once a friend passed the Orange sign and police told her to stop, she could not argue with the cops and in this way, I lost my interest on her as a girlfriend. Could you argue saying that you have passed the Orange sign and not the red sign with traffic police?

The legacy of the being

Thu Jul 24, 2014 7:08 am

Spontaneous manners on how to speak for ever in the hearts of Earthly aspects, is gained when the legacy is centered and spread in good hands and that is the division of goods.

Microcosms

Sun Jul 20, 2014 3:56 am

There were some people talking loud in my street, I had to stop Reading on line, then I awoke and felt lonely. I was better in my old house in another quarter, my room there has a view into a garden. From here the world looks big and from that room I had microcosms where peace existed.

The world is losing for images

Sat Jul 19, 2014 9:52 am

As the rusty face of the word confers the melodies of the sunrise which bath Earth with many golden temples and we can go inside the breathing stage of a scale of souvenirs because we are a selected poem of covered sorrows. To hold what we know as the dreaming of all souls existing, existed will exist to give grace for the surviving of the specie. The peacemakers shall continue while the word is losing for images.

The lovely wisdom of children

Sun Jul 13, 2014 8:17 am

In between the doors from those who enters and keeps the lovely wisdom of children, so near to sacred rooms of joy, playing and sending cartoons into the world, perhaps towers of continuity as beauty which ascends as the sublime. The task of a philosopher is the transmission of the being into the diversity of bridges between what is offered as the best pillow book and that is freedom...

The freedom of one burning idea

Sat Jul 12, 2014 6:00 pm

As every heated movement, the freedom of one burning idea is similar to the army of feelings which Giordano Bruno has found inside the Roman Catholic Church all along the century of himself but he has paid only because he paved the way to more factual insights who could rescue many humans as they tend to live out of tact. The correction of forgiveness often faces many human barriers, mainly in the formal tendency to seek escape in the crying cell of our assumptions. Something new had come with Wilhelm Reich and I wise to the crowd am the only human who can make rain without a Cloudbuster, having eye witnesses from Santo António Da Caparica in the year 2011 in Portugal. Alike Native American Indians, I fell on my own strange case and was caught by police. On my legacy on Orgonomy, I can serve the parameters where love, affection, feelings as generosity, work and devotion to this Earthly event upon the support of the human race. Suisse's have fed their nation during the World War II and now we could feed the world if a comprehensive mood would be carried by 1000 Cloudbuster in African deserts and from there globally. James DeMeo has the knowledge; do the American rulers will accept this evidence? We have to justify time and to be wiser than the skills of the media, to warm up like cats do, if we have pets with us and never to mystify a reason but to be reasonable in what is the river of good moods, like a fantastic castle of candy nerves named by children who sing with monuments of compliments. This is the quality of innocence. It can be done. Truth lies on the balance of divine measures.

To be at the top of the World

Sat Jul 05, 2014 8:02 pm

Brain activities could be something more than to be at the top of the world. Water can induce a flux of health little Indians with pony's delivering the good news of a new model of creation. This wish is as simple as complex ideas can dwell in the shape of the being and from this into eternity. Our plumed palm hands hold the first time that half of the world enters the mighty equations of Orgonometry. All gears run deeper when the next curve is one healing process with three methods: speech therapy, body relaxation, coach and the release of emotions.

The shining silence of human fate

Fri Jul 04, 2014 2:55 pm

An iron bird awakes to sing nearby its nest whose fragrance is sponsored by a colloquial moon. We could all be the movers and shakers of a good insight of beauty in the shining silence of human fate. To glue silence and to paste him into to the fading elements of discussion like birds, cats, pigeons, stars, plants, rocks, we all are beloved in the innate inner speech of the birth event which proceeds with ruins of a large sum of silenced fights. Motivation to this awake will take its steps in time, a certain refrain out of futility and inside the swimming thoughts which are electric sparks, jingling love signs to guaranty the future of our affect. We the triangle of ties and organized sleeping time as we date our fury all along beauty, to make it possible for time to be high above the indigo élan of days where the gestures are one possibility to be memorized into the look for love and only this energy is the royal moral of all existence. As certainty iron birds tend to coexist with the television skies in this digital age whose features are ferocious, denying to peasants to attend the soin.

Delight in the stillness

Thu May 08, 2014 4:20 am

Delight in the stillness, still seated while the humble voice ships the sun as vocation because nearby and whereas the nourishment produces wealth, the Confucianism teachings are of great importance. We have a Fender and a window to caress the passers, music reaches the feathers of birds as speed of a concealed zillion, a sum to confer as passage of births that are the golden area of 'totus tus'.

To confront life as a mission

Mon Apr 14, 2014 7:48 am

The long fidelity lies in sufficed triumphs which are balanced like a scarlet idea born from bliss. Going further in time with an expression of talent to defend the energy from the intervals of patience, the immediate escape from this situation is to confront life as a mission which allows silence to meet the spirituality of life.

Confucianism teachings

Mon Apr 14, 2014 6:44 am

Delight in the stillness, still seated while the humble voice ships the sun as vocation because nearby and whereas the nourishment produces wealth, the Confucianism teachings are of great importance. We have a Fender and a window to caress the passers, music reaches the feathers of birds as speed of a concealed zillion, a sum to confer as passage of births that are the golden area of 'totus tus'.

Hardcore regimes

Sun Mar 30, 2014 10:26 pm

To kill the representatives of hardcore regimes is not a solution.

Playing soccer with children

Sat Mar 29, 2014 2:35 pm

Playing soccer with children in the streets, makes us see how adults are socially positioned when they pass to observe.

The crowd solitude and its muscle

Wed Mar 26, 2014 8:41 am

A bullet proof intelligence does not exist because there are Sempiternal vocations which tend to adore beauty and not surveillance, one reason to refrain spying interventions lies on the crowd solitude and its muscle at times that she and me we twist the life of he.

This candy nerve in the heart of contentment

Tue Mar 25, 2014 8:36 am

When we do remember the reality of our promises towards others, we can conclude about the fact that needs are not temporary, the ties are present and they honor ourselves, it is up to the natural philosopher to learn and to teach about this candy nerve in the heart of contentment.

Free press is the key to all countries

Tue Mar 18, 2014 8:47 pm

In Finland, according to the research work, there is the freest press in the world, and if there is some corruption, we write and the politicians must be kicked off. Finland is on the top of the list of transparency, which ranks the countries and their corruption. Free press is the key to all countries.

Deepness

Tue Mar 18, 2014 7:38 pm

Deepness is affordable when the mind lies on accurate ascensions through levels of thought and reflection, allowing the individual to reach the inner voice with more truly sense than with immediacy. We have to be smarter than the skills of the media.

Wittgenstein

Mon Mar 17, 2014 8:51 pm

Wittgenstein decision to serve the Austrian army after writing ´Tratadus Logicus Philosophicus´ was a choice of a romantic soul.

Funny little ways

Mon Mar 17, 2014 7:03 pm

There is between minds, a connection which attracts people in daily dialogs, preceding dreams and thoughts about the ´leute´ that are part of us with the contact being deep or in funny little ways when we follow other people´s lives.

Swim in the sea swim inside me

Sun Mar 16, 2014 12:22 pm

The 25th century will be perhaps defined by a quality murmur of Earth while we have 500 years to adore the life of this time with good sense, a calm prudence which pretends to enter in the sea of time, therefore we must improve the quality of all, with the justice torch upon democracy balanced by organization.

Fundamental needs for our Earth

Fri Mar 14, 2014 9:01 am

Hydrogen, solar energy, wind energy are the solutions for the future but do the oil corporations are able to comprehend this fundamental need for our Earth?

Orgone units

Tue Mar 11, 2014 3:47 pm

There is no technology to film Orgone Units.

Concealing postures

Wed Feb 26, 2014 12:06 pm

Numerologists used to study during the sunset. Prudence confers her wisdom with a refined endurance so visible in the faces. We have to be dynamic in duos even safeguarding the ego, if it is autonomous with the senses for what peruses the singularity of a group. These meanings conceal postures of calculus, feelings like sweeties, time to create spaces where technology does not exist or will not exist ever. We cry salted tears waving our nostalgic traces when we wish to thrive for the decal of our innocence.

Tact

Tue Feb 25, 2014 1:45 pm

If you let somebody to do all the daily tasks, your tact will be out of touch.

The divine being of our nature

Tue Feb 25, 2014 11:57 am

The wild lizard looked at me, later in time throughout self-didacticism; I have learned how to heal mental problems. It was after my stroke. So much before I was an extreme physical individual doing all kind of sports. During dawn, I make my walks; no one is around except for cat's society and bird's society.

Mankind evolution is an expression of a multitude of tensions which could be healed by the analysts in this world and from the results, to shape the divine being of our nature.

The active brilliance of wealth

Sat Feb 22, 2014 8:08 pm

The myth from the eternal return finds in us pieces of creation sealing up the human will. The zeal for novels should begin by facing the facts: immediate circles of needs that are our daily output as pillar of the same organic measure as wealth.

Games without frontiers

Sat Feb 22, 2014 7:01 pm

The Sun will be extinguished, now we produce the precocious break of silence with games without frontiers.

A case of a lesbian

Mon Feb 17, 2014 10:28 am

I know a woman who had long fights with her father. When I met her for the first time, she was similar to Brigitte Bardot, some time had passed and she cut her hair, refusing to be pretty.

She liked to learn from me and I told her many secrets. After she had a degree in Fine Arts, she went to Berlin where she could live a homosexual relation with a woman and to be penetrated by one of them because in this way she would be solving the relation with her father with the lack of penis from her partner, she could castrate her father.

Sidereal mood

Mon Feb 17, 2014 8:25 am

For the songs which made the sunny days a delightful treasure with the sempiternal vocation in the exercise on how an embracing time among humans within a sidereal mood coexists in the good sense, in the good will.

Life

Sun Feb 16, 2014 8:56 am

Life is a something mysterious in the shape of energy.

Subtle ways to heal

Sat Feb 08, 2014 8:43 am

For 8 years I have healed one Architect with nervous anorexia, one Physician who was raped by her father at the age of 12 and one Psychologist who suffered from anxiety. All are now well. What I have found is that they were looking for the relief of symptoms and not seeking for the cure, so I had to be subtle.

Luck is for those who have courage

Fri Feb 07, 2014 9:23 pm

Trying to transform difficulties in a stimulus to go on and to have confidence in fate that always changes, transforming evil into good. Luck is for those who have courage.

The virginity of this age

Wed Feb 05, 2014 8:44 am

One rage becomes a tall emotion when an alakrab was shown in one girl's hands near the tank where I used to wash my own hands with blue soap. The rage becomes minus twenty beloved streams of history when the touch is one contemplation into the understanding of the honest life of Mr. Delfim and Mrs. Rosalina who were my adoptive grandparents and to whom with my first salary I spent 5 000 escudos (around 18USD-1988) in food because they were poor. The hand that handles the cradle, the babies on whom I held are well. Look for hope when the hope is you.

A personal momentum

Mon Feb 03, 2014 6:49 am

There is one woman which waits for the bus number 31 from 3 to 2 hours alone in the night. She looks at the electronic signal with the time for the waiting, gets excited when the bus is coming, then immediately she moves her fists and sings being in her own time, talking about her future and on sexuality. Something on her sexuality is related with her son, the pictures that she shows like a gift from her life; maybe at time of her son's birth was the great momentum of this woman, later being caught by psychiatry and now she saves time to be in freedom.

Humans eating cats due to starvation

Mon Feb 03, 2014 6:31 am

Romanian gypsies ate cats in my quarter because they were starving.

The Cosmic Calenture of Existence

Thu Jan 30, 2014 9:28 am

People should not depend on quotes because they would be confused but if you look at the pine for a long time you will become the pine. This is the cosmic calenture of silence which develops slowly on our inside.

Stars from the Planet Diamond

Tue Jan 28, 2014 4:20 pm

In the Fall of 2011, I saw the Planet Diamond emitting stars.

The deep eye

Fri Jan 24, 2014 8:55 am

Publicity is being an abuse on every financial sector throughout paper press, radio, tv, internet, street cars, trains, subway, placards and much more. We must avoid the eye from this contact, to read more as well to avoid futility.

A calm awareness

Wed Jan 22, 2014 4:06 pm

A colloquial speech presents many aspects of the body language, it can be known as a recall into the childhood distance till its appearance and it is also a fragrance of the present if well understood in the bowels of the diffused words.

Landscapes of existence

Tue Jan 21, 2014 10:51 pm

Alexander came in towers made of sand and the shape of a windy roar was so acoustic that both of them were uttering the sediments of will as iron and clearing out solutions for freedom.

Facebook, YouTube, Skype

Tue Jan 21, 2014 9:02 pm

Facebook is one tool who makes it easy for governments to control citizens, YouTube is a great robbery from copyrights and skype allows people to call worldwide alike others but the conversations are controlled as well.

Omniscience

Wed Jan 15, 2014 4:11 am

It is impossible for a mind to be omniscient.

Casual motility as showcase of our future

Fri Jan 10, 2014 9:15 am

I think that fate or casual motility points out the future, from each one we face the things which have the direction to support the orphans and the widows as well as the blind and the bums, this is what I do in my quarter.

Find a garden

Sat Dec 28, 2013 10:28 am

Find a garden in order to play ball games.

Cloudbuster and James DeMeo

Fri Dec 27, 2013 11:33 am

The Cloudbuster operations will not be done due to the lack of money funds, details can be found on OBRL by James DeMeo.
Finally, James DeMeo will use the Cloudbuster again, good news.
On his page, details can be found.
I had already warned about the importance of the Wilhelm Reich discovery for our days and now it will be possible again.

Technology

Thu Dec 26, 2013 2:27 pm

There is still no technology to appear as a new one as it matters computers and internet.

Christmas wishes for the ALF

Sat Dec 21, 2013 2:16 pm

I wish you all the best on your endeavor.
Christmas is one millenary event which most of the planet celebrate, therefore a reason to pray and to meditate for our beloved.

Sertralin and Sweden

Fri Dec 20, 2013 11:02 am

Sertralin is a chemic which is the most sold pill in Sweden for depression. Swedish blame the lack of sun, is it?

Translation business

Wed Dec 18, 2013 12:33 pm

The translation websites in order to work professionally demand a very low rate of income and demand a full dedication on this area of knowledge where the translators tend to enter in the author's mind and as consequence, they forget their own mind, a similar process to depersonalization.

Land

Wed Dec 18, 2013 6:13 am

The Seattle outburst from 1999 became an industry (see the economic value of Amazon where it is based), therefore we have to collect the flowers from the wise, to settle an industry of independence like the drummer of R.E.M. who quit playing in favor of agriculture, why land is so often forgotten?

Lula da Silva

Tue Dec 17, 2013 2:25 am

Lula da Silva doesn't know English, he wrote for The New York Times an article which can be found on their archives and which was translated from the Portuguese into English by a second person.

Pills for ADHD in adults

Thu Dec 12, 2013 12:23 am

The New England Journal of Medicine is introducing adds on its on-line edition concerning pills to treat ADHD in adults.

Plants longevity

Sat Dec 07, 2013 9:57 pm

People think that to have a Bonsai means longevity, well they are wrong, for to care of plants you reader would need a caring devotion day by day with eye contact.

Tribute to Shelley

Thu Dec 05, 2013 8:59 pm

Decal of purity on its epic powder towards sweet things.

Semper

Fri Nov 29, 2013 8:13 pm

Semper is a Latin word for always, it carries many meanings like fate or the choices we make or their consequences as tunes to the outcome of our goals.

Social Erection

Wed Nov 27, 2013 3:37 pm

Social Erection is like I have stated in my last publication, someone standing erected with sexual desire which often is a ghost in their personal lives, therefore it appears in this way. It is observable in train stations, bus stop and other public terminals. This will show how hidden sexual life among humans is being castrated by many factors such as anxiety born from the civilization as it is run nowadays.

Wilhelm Reich and television

Tue Nov 19, 2013 8:51 pm

Wilhelm Reich has never mentioned the word television in his entire production and research work.

Exercise of wisdom

Mon Nov 18, 2013 9:52 am

To cross borders either in body either in mind, means to have a certified guaranty among the current time and to safeguard him for the future by legal, logistic and human ways of exercising the testimony. To have a good quality of time, represents the measure of pleasure based in the body as escort of all the things we are concerned but it is the capacity of overcrossing these borders where we may feel with the exercise of wisdom.

A Castle of Cards

Sat Nov 16, 2013 2:41 pm

Making a castle of cards can enhance the hands skills for those who work with massages, the touch in general for the head, neck, face and all the body within its delicate points where a person can be in calm and away from negative thinking.

Alien disintegration, no knowledge

Fri Nov 15, 2013 3:24 am

There is no knowledge, nothing which can indicate what can save a human life from a hypothetical attempt on disintegration as condition.

French kissing

Wed Nov 13, 2013 11:33 am

Le roman "Mémoires d´une Jeune Fille Rangée", nous présente les dures expériences de Simone de Beauvoir dans le temps que son père est devenue désargenté. Simone est très intéressé dans son éducation et elle réussit en conquérir le monde avec ce roman. Elle est capable de faire son mieux avec ça force et rationalisme naturelle.

Inspiration

Tue Nov 12, 2013 11:34 pm

100 Greatest Lives, edited by John Allen is a wise book, we must learn to read in between the lines to capture the essence of its content beside the cult of history on which every biography does and it also inspires each one of us.

Wishes into a Russian senior

Fri Nov 08, 2013 8:30 pm

It is almost Christmas time, my wishes for you as always, have been clear as winter ice, the best is perhaps yet to come, therefore, do enter in calm deepening your senses inside you and far.

Emotional Plague by Charles Konia

Thu Nov 07, 2013 3:13 pm

The book, "The Emotional Plague" by Charles Konia, represents a tendency of an American Orgonomists in explaining the root of human evil but at the same time, defending the United States. He does not have a universal view of human evil neither he can achieve something new on Dr. Reich legacy, namely a creation either mechanic either scientific.

Coltsfoot

Wed Nov 06, 2013 9:31 pm

Coltsfoot has been used in herbal medicine and has been consumed as a food product with some confectionery products, such as Coltsfoot Rock. Tussilago farfara leaves have been used in the traditional Austrian medicine internally (as tea or syrup) or externally (directly applied) for treatment of disorders of the respiratory tract, skin, locomotor system, viral infections, flu, colds, fever, rheumatism and gout.

Metamorphosis

Tue Nov 05, 2013 1:58 am

Today the sparks were somehow lower than what they could be if the people would endorse their blues into a wave of some other sparks which probably would turn as green as the mantis knows so well how to cover inside nature, this is what I have found.

Food and ants

Mon Nov 04, 2013 10:59 pm

I could predict that food was going to be damaged by civilization, nowadays it is rare to see the vegetal kingdom existing with a sane and expansive atmosphere. Ants are one of the few species which survive into this civilization.

One example on how anyone can learn from a window

Sat Oct 26, 2013 1:45 am

Logistic is the ascension of matter towards the rise of feelings among two individuals and I wise to the crowd, could enhance beauty from a distant echo where cat´s society is well organized, that is what I could see for decades from my window. A tribute to Dona Maria Helena, known as the judge wife who was my friend and she also had shared with me this relation with cats.

Freud and future

Fri Oct 25, 2013 10:42 pm

Freud was a wise man, even if Reich was the most enlightened human of the 20th century, Freud was more rational and he could predict what is happening at the moment in the World. We have united efforts, to work endlessly, learn how to relax, to stay away from addictions, to make exercise, to practice philosophy: courage, autonomy, vigilance, lucidity.

Hillary Clinton

Fri Oct 25, 2013 6:49 pm

The criticize spirit must be induced in all.
Will Americans have on the White House a woman who was cheated by her husband?
Prevention is necessary, we must be political clean and not to swallow more plagues (see my critic on Konia´s book "The Emotional Plague" on Amazon).

A case of depression

Thu Oct 24, 2013 11:50 pm

One woman aged 44, has a severe depression which she sublimates with the writing of books, decoration of her house, simple things.
I had a long conversation and found a heavy feeling inside her. Solution pointed by her was God. This mystic thinking makes from her life instinct a way to cope with her traumas which she has not revealed. Her speech was sad with a mix of strength from her soul. This is the way society is going or maybe not, we shall see.

Patience

Thu Oct 24, 2013 12:09 am

Patience is necessary to endure the task the healers and free spirits, union is necessary. I forgive because it is the structure not the fundament.

To film dreams is a challenge for scientists

Wed Oct 23, 2013 9:36 pm

To film dreams will be a reality, work must take place.

Conduct as decal of love

Sat Sep 07, 2013 9:54 pm

Sweat is out from the pores, a water purifier can give more equalizing health like a social system could understand how organization of goods must be a union, the arguing of this secular issue lies on prudence, sensibility, execution of knowledge and devotion. No government can take the vocation from humans; they must coexist in conduct, ethic and coherence.

A Genius will appear in 200 years

Thu Sep 05, 2013 1:09 am

A Genius will appear in 200 years.

Nephew of Freud

Sat Aug 31, 2013 7:21 pm

The nephew of Freud was one of the responsible for the spreading of capitalism in the USA, concerning psychoanalysis history.

Wilhelm Reich and Noam Chomsky

Sat Aug 31, 2013 2:25 am

Professor Noam Chomsky has written me, that he could not understand my statement and he has "heard" of WR in the 50´s when he has read "The Mass Psychology of Fascism".

Wilhelm Reich and Noam Chomsky

Mon May 07, 2012 8:56 am

Dr. Wilhelm Reich on his book Character Analysis, wrote the following concerning language: ´ the beginning of living functioning lies much deeper than and beyond language, over and above he has its own modes of expressing movement which simply cannot be comprehended by words, answering Professor Chomsky with 20 years in advance of Noam´s time.

One case of racism

Thu Aug 22, 2013 1:56 pm

One German woman asked by me, if she knew about the scientific knowledge stated somewhere that black people were inferior but have a big penis. She said she knew about this but she wanted to be penetrated by an inferior specie, then she would take him into Germany to show this man into her friends.

To travel forever in the Outspace

Thu Aug 22, 2013 4:37 am

Maybe there will be time for humans to travel forever in the Outspace. There is enough time, we must listen the wise men and women in History in order to embrace a good cooperation with all. To fight the structures of today, to build ecological bridges worldwide, to seed and seed for an unknown period of time.

Yoga by Wilhelm Reich

Mon Aug 19, 2013 12:01 am

"Yoga: the sluggish epiphany of the medium" WR

Enter History with the care of poetry

Sat Aug 17, 2013 11:07 pm

To recruit one sweet element which sings among the leaves (for those who love secrets), then to articulate the state of our hair with the bright side of the medallion, a reality for those who expand another brick on the new walls. Back to what we expect, dignity, coming from a thousand goes, for the call whistling beauty, up in the lane, up on the road, inner life of the circle of working ideas to search in the humble with the glowing speed of love because the emotions on the heart can do anything but not with economical unions, so dear cosmic silence, enter history with the care of poetry.

Hypersensitive children

Fri Aug 02, 2013 7:30 pm

Hypersensitive children can feel what adults feel, not necessary their parents at times their perception has a dramatic or happy source of information from the outside. They need music to relax as a way to calm from the multitude of emotions. Parents must act in real time to defend the ego of the child into a clear design of the area where they move; it can be a bedroom or a car. Other therapies are a walk in the park like most parents do with them.

Human affect repressed by coercive medication

Fri Aug 02, 2013 10:41 am

One male adult was assaulted by conventional psychiatry at times he had a great physical power.
He is forced to take Fluanxol, once a month. With the inception of this substance, he trembles with induced attacks of Parkinson, then he takes Akineton to cope with Parkinson. The first consequence is the loss of memory.

It is a case of schizophrenia with caffeine and cigarettes as substitute for his need of affection which he had in his manhood, often girls used to approach him at his healthy condition. Now he is weak and he is dying slowly.

Memories hurt

Fri Aug 02, 2013 12:18 am

Memories hurt, someone said. The work upon the art of reflection requires a sacred ground where the green plants live long years in caring hands and there in the perfection of peace, the immanent parade of life is the period of time which we hold to keep it in eternity as we are all sacred and an ornament of the calenture, born from this.

Moral beauty

Mon Jul 29, 2013 8:12 am

Motility is the anticipation into the admissions of asperity which assures arguments of the citizens as motivation for the open dialogs whose gratitude finds eloquent dreams on those who dive on moral beauty.

The world is becoming more closed and not poetical

Tue Jul 23, 2013 4:06 am

Ethics should be known in the world. Why the academic world denies into the humble a free speech, why the skaters do not volunteer to the old who have rheumatologic difficulties, two examples on how media authority is leading everywhere as an assumption of knowledge not from wisdom. By sensibility I can heal any difficult problem with someone's flow of energy or even the great strains of the world situation, I made contacts with everybody from the intellectual influent torrent of thoughts and new ideas, since the field of environment, pollution, legal protection into the fragile, nature, wars, food and so forth but the will for their own power has selected their own society, so the world is becoming more closed and not poetical.

Yesterday (like nostalgia would say),

Tue Jul 23, 2013 3:38 am

Yesterday (like nostalgia would say), I saw many bad news about how the kings and queens fool the ghosts of a smile, so similar to what photographers do in small villages with the population despite the immanent good will of the peasants.

Somehow is a decay, how humans are away from themselves, maybe because their will is a hate picture so well hidden.

How traditional psychiatry works

Sun Jul 21, 2013 4:10 am

I had to call the emergency health line in order to take my father to hospital because he could not express what he was going inside his mind, he was getting thinner each day, I and my mother had to go into his house every day to feed him; so we went. The man from the health emergency told: "today, we only have such cases". The hospital was crowded, I was stressed waiting at the sun. They gave him Diazepam, then he went into a mental hospital. There I spoke with one woman which was psychiatrist in charge of his case and told her:" I had not the power to take my father into Switzerland to see Dr. Alberto Foglia which practices Medical Orgonomy so I came here, can you speak and make him psychoanalysis?" There was a psychiatrist student who had never heard of Wilhelm Reich and Alexander Lowen, he was observing the interview. I made my analysis of my father, the psychiatrist was interested but soon she withdrew from my efforts. They gave Haldol to my father, he was zombified, I have protested and was asked if I was a psychiatrist. One week later he was free. I say free because he was in one prison.
Now my father comes to me and my mother each weekend, he stays in calm, thinking at a chair where he expresses his thoughts and ideas.
That is how traditional psychiatry works in Portugal.

Foundation

Mon Jul 08, 2013 3:45 pm

This web site together with more workers and volunteers on Alexander Lowen legacy, is going perhaps to slow and where do the donations, workshops, discussions, sales of books have a direct effect on the world?

SCHIZOPHRENIA A Nonexistent Disease by Lawrence Stevens,

Wed Jul 03, 2013 8:08 pm

Schizophrenia is the result of ocular repression with panic and splitting (See Man in the Trap, page 141 by Elsworth Baker).

SCHIZOPHRENIA A Nonexistent Disease by Lawrence Stevens, J.D

Sat May 12, 2012 1:21 am

The word "schizophrenia" has a scientific sound that seems to give it inherent credibility and a charisma that seems to dazzle people. In his book Molecules of the Mind - The Brave New Science of Molecular Psychology, University of Maryland journalism professor Jon Franklin calls schizophrenia and depression "the two classic forms of mental illness" (Dell Publishing Co., 1987, p. 119). According to the cover article in the July 6, 1992 Time magazine, schizophrenia is the "most devilish of mental illnesses" (p. 53). This Time magazine article says "fully a quarter of the nation's hospital beds are occupied by schizophrenia patients" (p. 55). Books and articles like these and the facts to which they refer (such as a quarter of hospital beds being occupied by so-called schizophrenics) delude most people into believing there really is a disease called schizophrenia. Schizophrenia is one of the great myths of our time.

In his book Schizophrenia - The Sacred Symbol of Psychiatry, psychiatry professor Thomas S. Szasz, M.D., says "There is, in short, no such thing as schizophrenia" (Syracuse University Press, 1988, p. 191). In the Epilogue of their book Schizophrenia - Medical Diagnosis or Moral Verdict? Theodore R. Sarbin, Ph.D., a psychology professor at the University of California at Santa Cruz who spent three years working in mental hospitals, and James C. Mancuso, Ph.D., a psychology professor at the State University of New York at Albany, say: "We have come to the end of our journey. Among other things, we have tried to establish that the schizophrenia model of unwanted conduct lacks credibility. The analysis directs us ineluctably to the conclusion that schizophrenia is a myth" (Pergamon Press, 1980, p. 221). In his book Against Therapy, published in 1988, Jeffrey Masson, Ph.D., a psychoanalyst, says "There is a heightened awareness of the dangers inherent in labeling somebody with a disease category like schizophrenia, and many people are beginning to realize that there is no such entity" (Atheneum, p. 2). Rather than being a bona-fide disease, so-called schizophrenia is a nonspecific category which includes almost everything a human being can do, think, or feel that is greatly disliked by other people or by the so-called schizophrenics themselves. There are few so-called mental illnesses that have not at one time or another been called schizophrenia. Because schizophrenia is a term that covers just about everything a person can think or do which people greatly dislike, it is hard to define objectively. Typically, definitions of schizophrenia are vague or inconsistent with each other. For example, when I asked a physician who was the Assistant Superintendent of a state mental hospital to define the term schizophrenia for me, he with all seriousness replied, "split personality - that's the most popular definition." In contrast, a pamphlet published by the National Alliance for the Mentally Ill titled "What Is Schizophrenia?" says "Schizophrenia is not a split personality". In her book Schiz-o-phre-nia: Straight Talk for Family and Friends, published in 1985, Maryellen Walsh says "Schizophrenia is one of the most misunderstood diseases on the planet. Most people think that it means having a split personality. Most people are wrong. Schizophrenia is not a splitting of the personality into multiple parts" (Warner Books, p. 41). The American Psychiatric Association's (APA's) Diagnostic and Statistical Manual of Mental Disorders (Second Edition), also known as DSM-II, published in 1968, defined schizophrenia as "characteristic disturbances of thinking, mood, or behavior" (p. 33). A difficulty with such a definition is it is so broad just about anything people dislike or consider abnormal, i.e., any so-called mental illness, can fit within it. In the Foreword to DSM-II, Ernest M. Gruenberg, M.D., D.P.H., Chairman of the American Psychiatric Association's Committee on Nomenclature, said: "Consider, for example, the mental disorder labeled in the Manual as 'schizophrenia,' ... Even if it had tried, the Committee could not establish agreement about what this disorder is" (p. ix). The third edition of the APA's Diagnostic and Statistical Manual of Mental Disorders, published in 1980, commonly called DSM-III, was also quite candid about the vagueness of the term. It said: "The limits of the concept of Schizophrenia are unclear" (p. 181). The revision published in 1987, DSM-III-R, contains a similar statement: "It should be noted that no single feature is invariably present or seen only in Schizophrenia" (p. 188). DSM-III-R also says this about a related diagnosis, Schizoaffective Disorder: "The term Schizoaffective Disorder has been used in many different ways since it was first introduced as a subtype of Schizophrenia, and represents one of the most confusing and controversial concepts in psychiatric nosology" (p. 208).

Particularly noteworthy in today's prevailing intellectual climate in which mental illness is considered to have biological or chemical causes is what DSM-III-R, says about such physical causes of this catch-all concept of schizophrenia: It says a diagnosis of schizophrenia "is made only when it cannot be established that an organic factor initiated and maintained the disturbance" (p. 187). Underscoring this definition of "schizophrenia" as non-biological is the 1987 edition of The Merck Manual of Diagnosis and Therapy, which says a (so-called) diagnosis of schizophrenia is made only when the behavior in question is "not due to organic mental disorder" (p. 1532).

Contrast this with a statement by psychiatrist E. Fuller Torrey, M.D., in his book Surviving Schizophrenia: A Family Manual, published in 1988. He says "Schizophrenia is a brain disease, now definitely known to be such" (Harper & Row, p. 5). Of course,[color=#00FF00] if schizophrenia is a brain disease, then it is organic. However, the official definition of schizophrenia maintained and published by the American Psychiatric Association in its Diagnostic and Statistical Manual of Mental Disorders for many years specifically excluded organically caused conditions from the definition of schizophrenia. Not until the publication of DSM-IV in 1994 was the exclusion for biologically caused conditions removed from the definition of schizophrenia. In Surviving Schizophrenia, Dr. Torrey acknowledges "the prevailing psychoanalytic and family interaction theories of schizophrenia which were prevalent in American psychiatry" (p. 149) which would seem to account for this.

In the November 10, 1988 issue of Nature, genetic researcher Eric S. Lander of Harvard University and M.I.T. summarized the situation this way: "The late US Supreme Court Justice Potter Stewart declared in a celebrated obscenity case that, although he could not rigorously define pornography, `I know it when I see it'. Psychiatrists are in much the same position concerning the diagnosis of schizophrenia. Some 80 years after the term was coined to describe a devastating condition involving a mental split among the functions of thought, emotion and behaviour, there remains no universally accepted definition of schizophrenia" (p. 105).

According to Dr. Torrey in his book Surviving Schizophrenia, so-called schizophrenia includes several widely divergent personality types. Included among them are paranoid schizophrenics, who have "delusions and/or hallucinations" that are either "persecutory" or "grandiose"; hebephrenic schizophrenics, in whom "well-developed delusions are usually absent"; catatonic schizophrenics who tend to be characterized by "posturing, rigidity, stupor, and often mutism" or, in other words, sitting around in a motionless, nonreactive state (in contrast to paranoid schizophrenics who tend to be suspicious and jumpy); and simple schizophrenics, who exhibit a "loss of interest and initiative" like the catatonic schizophrenics (though not as severe) and unlike the paranoid schizophrenics have an "absence of delusions or hallucinations" (p. 77). The 1968 edition of the American Psychiatric Association's Diagnostic and Statistical Manual of Mental Disorders, DSM-II, indicates a person who is very happy (experiences "pronounced elation") may be defined as schizophrenic for this reason ("Schizophrenia, schizo-affective type, excited") or very unhappy ("Schizophrenia, schizo-affective type, depressed")(p. 35), and the 1987 edition, DSM-III-R, indicates a person can be "diagnosed" as schizophrenic because he displays neither happiness nor sadness ("no signs of affective expression")(p. 189), which Dr. Torrey in his book calls simple schizophrenia ("blunting of emotions")(p. 77). According to psychiatry professor Jonas Robitscher, J.D., M.D., in his book The Powers of Psychiatry, people who cycle back and forth between happiness and sadness, the so-called manic-depressives or suffers of "bipolar mood disorder", may also be called schizophrenic: "Many cases that are diagnosed as schizophrenia in the United States would be diagnosed as manic-depressive illness in England or Western Europe" (Houghton Mifflin, 1980, p. 165.) So the supposed "symptoms" or defining characteristics of "schizophrenia" are broad indeed, defining people as having some kind of schizophrenia because they have delusions or do not, hallucinate or do not, are jumpy or catatonic, are happy, sad, or neither happy nor sad, or cycling back and forth between happiness and sadness. Since no physical causes of "schizophrenia" have been found, as we'll soon see, this "disease" can be defined only in terms of its "symptoms", which as you can see are what might be called ubiquitous. As attorney Bruce Ennis says in his book Prisoners of Psychiatry: "schizophrenia is such an all-inclusive term and covers such a large range of behavior that there are few people who could not, at one time or another, be considered schizophrenic" (Harcourt Brace Jovanovich, Inc., 1972, p. 22). People who are obsessed with certain thoughts or who feel compelled to perform certain behaviors, such as washing their hands repeatedly, are usually considered to be suffering from a separate psychiatric disease called "obsessive-compulsive disorder". However, people with obsessive thoughts or compulsive behaviors have also been called schizophrenic (e.g., by Dr. Torrey in his book Surviving Schizophrenia, pp. 115-116).

In Surviving Schizophrenia, Dr. Torrey quite candidly concedes the impossibility of defining what "schizophrenia" is. He says: "The definitions of most diseases of mankind has been accomplished. ... In almost all diseases there is something which can be seen or measured, and this can be used to define the disease and separate it from nondisease states. Not so with schizophrenia! To date we have no single thing which can be measured and from which we can then say: Yes, that is schizophrenia. Because of this, the definition of the disease is a source of great confusion and debate" (p. 73). What puzzles me is how to reconcile this statement of Dr. Torrey's with another he makes in the same book, which I quoted above and which appears more fully as follows: "Schizophrenia is a brain disease, now definitely known to be such. It is a real scientific and biological entity, as clearly as diabetes, multiple sclerosis, and cancer are scientific and biological entities" (p. 5). How can it be known schizophrenia is a brain disease when we do not know what schizophrenia is?

The truth is that the label schizophrenia, like the labels pornography or mental illness, indicates disapproval of that to which the label is applied and nothing more. Like "mental illness" or pornography, "schizophrenia" does not exist in the sense that cancer and heart disease exist but exists only in the sense that good and bad exist. As with all other so-called mental illnesses, a diagnosis of "schizophrenia" is a reflection of the speaker's or "diagnostician's" values or ideas about how a person "should" be, often coupled with the false (or at least unproven) assumption that the disapproved thinking, emotions, or behavior results from a biological abnormality. Considering the many ways it has been used, it's clear "schizophrenia" has no particular meaning other than "I dislike it." Because of this, I lose some of my respect for mental health professionals when I hear them use the word schizophrenia in a way that indicates they think it is a real disease. I do this for the same reason I would lose respect for someone's perceptiveness or intellectual integrity after hearing him or her admire the emperor's new clothes. While the layman definition of schizophrenia, internally inconsistent, may make some sense, using the term "schizophrenia" in a way that indicates the speaker thinks it is a real disease is tantamount to admitting he doesn't know what he is talking about.

Many mental health "professionals" and other "scientific" researchers do however persist in believing "schizophrenia" is a real disease. They are like the crowds of people observing the emperor's new clothes, unable or unwilling to see the truth because so many others before them have said it is real. A glance through the articles listed under "Schizophrenia" in Index Medicus, an index of medical periodicals, reveals how widespread the schizophrenia myth has become. And because these "scientists" believe "schizophrenia" is a real disease, they try to find physical causes for it. As psychiatrist William Glasser, M.D., says in his book Positive Addiction, published in 1976: "Schizophrenia sounds so much like a disease that prominent scientists delude themselves into searching for its cure" (Harper & Row, p. 18). This is a silly endeavor, because these supposedly prominent scientists can't define "schizophrenia" and accordingly don't know what they are looking for.

According to three Stanford University psychiatry professors, "two hypotheses have dominated the search for a biological substrate of schizophrenia." They say these two theories are the transmethylation hypothesis of schizophrenia and the dopamine hypothesis of schizophrenia. (Jack D. Barchas, M.D., et al., "Biogenic Amine Hypothesis of Schizophrenia", appearing in Psychopharmacology: From Theory to Practice, Oxford University Press, 1977, p. 100.) The transmethylation hypothesis was based on the idea that "schizophrenia" might be caused by "aberrant formation of methylated amines" similar to the hallucinogenic pleasure drug mescaline in the metabolism of so-called schizophrenics. After reviewing various attempts to verify this theory, they conclude: "More than two decades after the introduction of the transmethylation hypothesis, no conclusions can be drawn about its relevance to or involvement in schizophrenia" (p. 107).

Columbia University psychiatry professor Jerrold S. Maxmen, M.D., succinctly describes the second major biological theory of so-called schizophrenia, the dopamine hypothesis, in his book The New Psychiatry, published in 1985: "...many psychiatrists believe that schizophrenia involves excessive activity in the dopamine-receptor system...the schizophrenic's symptoms result partially from receptors being overwhelmed by dopamine" (Mentor, pp. 142 & 154). But in the article by three Stanford University psychiatry professors I referred to above they say "direct confirmation that dopamine is involved in schizophrenia continues to elude investigators" (p. 112). In 1987 in his book Molecules of the Mind Professor Jon Franklin says "The dopamine hypothesis, in short, was wrong" (p. 114).

In that same book, Professor Franklin aptly describes efforts to find other biological causes of so-called schizophrenia: "As always, schizophrenia was the index disease. During the 1940s and 1950s, hundreds of scientists occupied themselves at one time and another with testing samples of schizophrenics' bodily reactions and fluids. They tested skin conductivity, cultured skin cells, analyzed blood, saliva, and sweat, and stared reflectively into test tubes of schizophrenic urine. The result of all this was a continuing series of announcements that this or that difference had been found. One early researcher, for instance, claimed to have isolated a substance from the urine of schizophrenics that made spiders weave cockeyed webs. Another group thought that the blood of schizophrenics contained a faulty metabolite of adrenaline that caused hallucinations. Still another proposed that the disease was caused by a vitamin deficiency. Such developments made great newspaper stories, which generally hinted, or predicted outright, that the enigma of schizophrenia had finally been solved. Unfortunately, in light of close scrutiny none of the discoveries held water" (p. 172).

Other efforts to prove a biological basis for so-called schizophrenia have involved brain-scans of pairs of identical twins when only one is a supposed schizophrenic. They do indeed show the so-called schizophrenic has brain damage his identical twin lacks. The flaw in these studies is the so-called schizophrenic has inevitably been given brain-damaging drugs called neuroleptics as a so-called treatment for his so-called schizophrenia. It is these brain-damaging drugs, not so-called schizophrenia, that have caused the brain damage. Anyone "treated" with these drugs will have such brain damage. Damaging the brains of people eccentric, obnoxious, imaginative, or mentally disabled enough to be called schizophrenic with drugs (erroneously) believed to have anti schizophrenic properties is one of the saddest and most indefensible consequences of today's widespread belief in the myth of schizophrenia.

In The New Harvard Guide to Psychiatry, published in 1988, Seymour S. Kety, M.D., Professor Emeritus of Neuroscience in Psychiatry, and Steven Matthysse, Ph.D., Associate Professor of Psychobiology, both of Harvard Medical School, say "an impartial reading of the recent literature does not provide the hoped-for clarification of the catecholamine hypotheses, nor does compelling evidence emerge for other biological differences that may characterize the brains of patients with mental disease" (Harvard University Press, p. 148).

Belief in biological causes of so-called mental illness, including schizophrenia, comes not from science but from wishful thinking or from desire to avoid coming to terms with the experiential/environmental causes of people's misbehavior or distress. The repeated failure of efforts to find biological causes of so-called schizophrenia suggests "schizophrenia" belongs only in the category of socially/culturally unacceptable thinking or behavior rather than in the category of biology or "disease" where many people place it.

THE AUTHOR, Lawrence Stevens, is a lawyer whose practice has included representing psychiatric "patients". His pamphlets are not copyrighted. Feel free to make copies.

A MOTHERS SACRIFICE FILLED WITH UNCONDITIONAL LOVE

Wed May 29, 2013 11:20 pm

A MOTHERS SACRIFICE FILLED WITH UNCONDITIONAL LOVE

My mom only had one eye. I hated her... she was such an embarrassment
She cooked for students & teachers to support the family
There was this one day during elementary school where my mom came to say hello to me
I was so embarrassed. How could she do this? to me
I ignored her, threw her a hateful look and ran out The next day at school one of my classmates said, \"EEEE, your mom only has \"!one eye
I wanted to bury myself. I also wanted my mom to just disappear
so I confronted her that day and said, \" If you're only going to make me a laughing stock, why \"!!!?don't you just die
My mom did not ...respond
I didn't even stop to think for a second about what I had said, because I was full of anger
I was oblivious to her feelings
I wanted out of that house, and have nothing to do with her
So I studied real hard, got a chance to go to Singapore to study
Then, I got married. I bought a house of my own. I had kids of my own
I was happy with my life, my kids and the comforts
Then one day, my mother came to visit me
She hadn't seen me in years and she didn't even meet her grandchildren
When she stood by the door, my children laughed at her, and I yelled at her for coming over uninvited
I screamed at her, \"How dare you come to my house and scare my children! \" \"!!!GET OUT OF HERE! NOW

And to this, my mother quietly answered, \"Oh, I'm so sorry. I may have gotten the wrong address," and she disappeared .out of sight

One day, a letter regarding a school reunion came to my house in Singapore

So I lied to my wife that I was going on a business trip

After the reunion, I went to the old shack just out of curiosity

My neighbors said that she died

I did not shed a single tear

They handed me a letter that she had wanted me to have

My dearest son" I think of you all the time. I'm sorry that I came to Singapore and scared your children

I was so glad when I heard you were coming for the reunion

But I may not be able to even get out of bed to see you

I'm sorry that I was a constant embarrassment to you when you were growing up

You see... when you were very little, you got into an accident, and lost your eye

As a mother, I couldn't stand watching you having .to grow up with one eye. So I gave you mine

I was so proud of my son who was seeing a whole new world for me, in my place, with that eye,

With my love to you
Your mother

Calm

Wed Apr 17, 2013 11:05 am

I was observing a blue pigeon walking in the street, we were in calm and a woman was standing in the front building holding a baby to attend our calm.

The need for a World government

Sat Apr 06, 2013 12:59 pm

The existence of a World government could balance global situations more than the existing of states one by one. The United Nations influence can help to trigger this aspect of human condition in order to improve the World for all species and of course to inspire the words which are the commanders of societies.

Girl with Asperger takes Risperdal

Thu Apr 04, 2013 2:50 am

I know a teenager with Asperger who takes Risperdal, she reads many books beside her school duties. The parents of this girl have low wages but she is one happy girl even with the chemical flow and the economic situation because she trusts her soul. She has made me a delicious cake at the time of my birthday.

Soin for our personal history

Thu Mar 14, 2013 3:53 am

The media are responsible for the amount of information which makes people from all ages to forget their personal history, following a truant perusing of the 'soin'. Naturally side by side, the hosting of intelligence, logistic, physical shape provides elements of harmony in the organization of a healthy sentimentalism towards the sweet things.

Touch

Tue Mar 12, 2013 10:48 pm

The temperature of the body is a conscious liberation which triggers thought from human to human when its talking falls wide open to seek for the anima of those who are engaged in the touch. We can do it for ourselves in distinct manners whose laces are traces in the lucidity of the personal discoveries of each human philosophical system on where we can enter with the care of the first flash in Eden.

Seeds of love for the 22nd century

Tue Mar 12, 2013 10:21 pm

In the 22nd century, the world will be the tissue of a moving concern into health. It is time now to seed.

Food for thought?

Sun Mar 10, 2013 1:19 am

"Clinical nutrition is nutrition of patients in health care. Clinical in this sense refers to the management of patients, not only outpatients at clinics, but also, and mainly, inpatients in hospitals. It incorporates mainly the scientific fields of nutrition and dietetics. It aims to keep a healthy energy balance in patients, as well as providing sufficient amounts other nutrients such as protein, vitamins, minerals." My question for the bioenergetics community is about the wide field of food which is directly in concern of the body and its specific role in our lives.

Pansexuality

Fri Feb 15, 2013 6:32 am

While I was working in admissions into the pansexuality of what is the precaution into a clear amusement, my wishes were the open treasure of moral beauty. I could undertake human dust, to command imagination by a large gain of truth by scenes of virtue; the brightest revelation of love is a petal whispering in the legacy of wisdom. The grace of this specie is a case of trust, it exists to peruse life.

Multiple sclerosis treatment

Tue Feb 05, 2013 8:53 pm

Multiple sclerosis hereditary mutation of the gene can be identified in order to create a chemical compound which allows the patient to improve and to get rid of the situation. The sexual clinic history of the patient is necessary at its full length (complete). Gathering both, the patient will be healthy and this is applicable into all ages.

Peter Reich

Wed Jan 23, 2013 9:10 pm

4 views on Peter Reich and 15 000 on junk posts, INCREDIBLE HOW THE EMOTIONAL PLAGUE ATTACKS HUMANS

Thu Jan 17, 2013 7:45 pm

Areas of Interest

My current research focuses on the impacts of global environmental change on terrestrial ecosystems. This includes effects of climate change, elevated atmospheric carbon dioxide, other air pollutants, land use/management, fire and biotic invasion on health, biodiversity, and sustainability of forest and grassland ecosystems both in Minnesota and globally. This work simultaneously attempts to bridge the fields of physiological, community, ecosystem, landscape, and global ecology. We tend to focus on the broad ecotone of central North America, where boreal forests, northern hardwood forests, oak woodlands/savannas, and grasslands converge and mix. However, we are involved in projects that address similar themes and issues in many other biomes and geographic locations, including work in several other continents (Australia, Europe, South America).

Neurasthenia cure

Thu Jan 17, 2013 12:36 pm

The imaging of the brain tissue at the time of a neural explosion will make it possible to understand the dynamic of the genes of a person with neurasthenia. These elements which are moving among the vessels can be handled with the calm fluency of the post event located in the brain with the help of the stimulus speech, television sport events by paying attention into the tactics and with the results of the inner talk towards the ego on daily routines such as walking, cleaning, reading, communicating and many others.
I had good results with speech therapy, technology on this matter doesn't exist.

*None of the above information is meant to substitute for the advice of a doctor. If you are experiencing any of the abovementioned mental or physical disturbances, you should consult your physician.

Human wish

Mon Jan 14, 2013 7:24 am

Roving the dust as path into a potent love while the kindled rapture of memories are intense sayings of dew drops dissolved in spheres of a true identity, this is why nature is observing humans as a piece of work in the plates where we discuss that a loud appeal of all and it stops in time in order to justify the echoes of the same shore where our wings rise into the lightning skies for the sublime to a better understanding for what is stands as a human wish.

Appeal for a Written resume of the ALF Christmas gift

Wed Dec 26, 2012 10:21 am

Someone can make a written resume from the Alexander Lowen Foundation Christmas gift? My neighbors make tremendous noise and I sleep not so well during my leisure time.

Timeless love

Mon Dec 24, 2012 7:38 pm

From experience to state eloquently in written words, showed me that I could activate many people. My physical healing had no books, it was a blessing care into others. I have had spent 40 years healing people. Someone told that the most important thing is not the combat but the preparation into it. You can try Ginger and your mind with the song of coherence on what it concerns the past: how can we learn from them as people, how to give new energy into the realm of love? Meditation enhances into feeble reactions the history of rage and all the rainbows are like poetry, one divine masculine which does not know yuppies, shapes the world like Michael Landon, revamps the perceiving of the second person in the eye movement of wisdom. When you return home from a distant shore, remember to tell yourself: "this could be my memorable taste of freedom", then the Ginger cleans the organism inside the apartment where most of the western world lives, reads, plays, studies, plans. This actual condition is what we have. If dreams can advise you, then dream in peace, no word can hurt the wisdom of magic while the stones were a playful time with the peasants from Lordelo from Vila Real. Nothing could be something if the feeling is right and those kids run in grace, they know how a dog can recognize the beloved one year later in calm, only by the smell. That was Zig my brave dog and the wisdom which rings the bells into what is a rich logic from who rents time to become a narrator in the immanent pansexuality and leaves successors for the world because we must paint the love teachings before this picture goes, only this makes sense.

Logistic on bioenergetics

Sat Dec 15, 2012 6:50 pm

Dear Yaniv,

Maybe to have a place a logistic structure like hospitals have, with mobile for emergencies and a therapy center according to Alexander Lowen teachings first there in the united states and throughout the world like the Forum user, Marini in Brazil.

I have read one boy or man in great affliction on an open topic and I could advise him and for those who suffer the importance of logistic and of Alexander Lowen students to practice, teach, heal and advice.

A php Forum has many limitations but it is a start, a good one. There are topics with 7 000 views. Maybe people never read Alexander Lowen from those 7 000. So, I think it is a matter of time and organization like the American College of Orgonomy is doing.

Thank you for your sympathy,

Cordially,

Eduardo

Nature is a language can't you read?

Fri Dec 14, 2012 4:01 am

It seems to exist a need to express time with worldly sport events which make people to forget about nature and the nature of people becomes Olympic with the lift of this torch on the games people play but it is a fact that nature takes hold of people so it is a good seating place the happy realm of being close to the parcel of land where the relaxation is possible.

Dreams will be filmed in the future

Wed Dec 12, 2012 7:27 am

In the future, it will be possible to film the dreams of humans.

The autonomous ego

Sat Dec 08, 2012 5:35 pm

Seated to seal blood on May the 31th of 1995, the tree had hold us while the difference of our bodies was the reason to attend another call inside the logic of love, somehow a leap on the road where we had been for so many times now the bridge holds the long fidelity towards the dichotomy of the assembly of the life when she is one unity.
My father prefers to see, to feel rather than to write. He took me into so many places with his white car, so brave on the Portuguese incursions across the roads far from my first home even if I had many homes, that house was my real home. There I created at the age of 12 the social or individual praxis of the autonomous ego. Later in Germany a group of rioters called themselves autonomous, there and here the responsibility on any discovery especially when she and me do not depend on the heritage of the facts which produce means to begin the love and the gain of emotions inside the realm of innocence since March till the good kingdom of faith.

My Christmas wishes for the Alexander Lowen Foundation

Tue Dec 04, 2012 8:49 pm

My Christmas wishes for the Alexander Lowen Foundation, their supporters, friends, readers, relatives.
May Alexander Lowen teachings can play an active role on the education of the civilization with humor and seriousness as condition of what is felt

because what is felt is of our concern (Epikur).

Vizir
(Eduardo Alexandre Pinto)

A case of a Finnish woman in Portugal

Mon Dec 03, 2012 3:56 am

One of the reasons is that when I was there as European and I get my first baby there, you know what they say to me they say that I should go home to Finland because they can't help mi there they have money only of them own people...time I live there with baby I truly struggle and the way Portuguese people think they a somehow better than me who don't speak Portuguese is also very stupid, did I tell you how they treat mi anytime I try and work there...they refuse to talk to me ´nada´(nothing) of holly day/night time because I speak English and anything I do they behave like they do it better...there was times when I was very sad I has my baby and no woman on our street want to be my friend they only say mi hi how are you and good day and good bye, that all, one time I was very lonely and I when to shop there was this one nice looking lady I see there working before and I which she could be my friend and talk to me, so I when there and pay something small just so that I can say word with her and ask her to be my friend, when I reach her in the glue/line and she smile and great me and I open my mouth to speak then all the sudden woman behind me, my neighbor she live in the second house near me shout from my back very loud " don't speak to her she's not Portuguese, she don't speak the language" this she say with Portuguese...´não fala nada com ela ela não fala português´(don´t talk with her she does not talk Portuguese) or something like that and ges what happened that sweet woman who I which to be my friend she was Indian lady or something she turned her head down and didn't look on mi again I stayed silent (because I was so deep sad and very lonely) ´eu falo pouco´I speak little)...but she didn't answer I look back in the line and no fucking people even look at me...like I was sickness they want to get read of...this is how they treat me in Portugal, why should I hear them cry...when they didn't care if i am doing crying lonely or dead lonely...

Wilhelm Reich and Einstein

Fri Nov 30, 2012 3:48 am

The only explanation Einstein gave to Reich for not wanting to cooperate with him was that one of Einstein's assistants gave a different explanation of the temperature difference phenomenon. Einstein accepted that different explanation. The entire Reich-Einstein correspondence is included in Reich's autobiographical book American Odyssey.

The bioelectrical investigation of sexuality and anxiety

Thu Nov 29, 2012 1:50 pm

The death instinct is not "mute", but instead what is called the death instinct, namely the retraction of life energy, manifests itself clearly as anxiety. If chronic anxiety processes were to accelerate dying, it would not prove the existence of a death instinct, but rather of the anti-life effect of sexual inhibition, because the suppression of the parasympathetic function enhances the sympathetic function; i.e. the process of dying out, becoming enervated, and "crawling back into the self" . in short, the abatement of all life functions.

Totus Tus

Wed Nov 28, 2012 4:13 am

In the Spring of 1997, I entered into a gipsy ghetto, invited a child to take a ride on my bicycle and we had fun riding through Lisbon. Later we stopped in a garden of Campo Grande and relaxed on the grass, watching people having amusement in the lake, near the Caleidoscópio shopping center where Mr. Ricardo Balona has worked in the library.
Later in time this child and others grew and turned out as bandits which means that if the work with children is not made in full time like comrades

do, they get lost in the mime behavior of adults, being a wall street wacko or a smuggler of endless schemes on what the vacuum says nothing at all.

About Writers

Tue Nov 27, 2012 1:29 pm

Writers failed to understand the natural love among humans and they spread negative unselected pieces of things which any sharpened detector knows well. The scientific authors have my great consideration because they save lives by prevention on this planet. Wild Life is being guarded carefully or maybe not, seldom it appears news about wolfs for example and if so they are forgotten in time, wolfs and the beavers (maybe to left them on their peace is the best).

When words are like an Asiatic shore and Pierre de Lotti (a sailor) embraces the readings of the things his adventures produced into the romantic Oceans, things that are alive as spots in one loyal Dalmatian. To cross what is seldom is like being another summer in the Ocean bioluminescence with calm wise turtles passing through decades willing for peace and up above, the weather in its languor as a sociologist would try to be the parish the decal of this faith on the infinite as one child being found. As promise into the inspiring people which carry carpets and sell secrets to obtain from the Poet the necessary loop to camp his willing mind into a good bright portion of the same principle of adventure either from the seas, either from the human heart. Temperament holds the perfect kiss into joy and bliss.

The reality of Bahamas

Tue Nov 27, 2012 3:54 am

To the Bahamas come vacationists with money to rest, to take the sun, enjoy and to spend money. The simple citizens of Bahamas work because to live. Any persons have own business, any have 2 or 3 jobs. I live with my daughter. For us the life here is difficult.

Solidarity was the resident word for our friendship because what Lech Walesa did, meant to be serious but it failed.

Eye problems and technology

Sat Nov 24, 2012 11:23 am

Eye problems are a reality among youth and adults due to the use of the actual technology.

Medicaments in the future

Fri Nov 23, 2012 10:35 pm

In the future, medicaments will be produced according to each individual organism.

Humans spend 4 hours per day around a vehicle in a year

Fri Nov 09, 2012 11:03 pm

Roads, traffic jam, gas station, parking places, garages, cleaning, races, tv, taxes, exams, taxis and much more.

Farrar Strauss & Giroux and the Judas Kiss

Wed Nov 07, 2012 7:42 am

In my dreams I was going with a female friend inside a shop, there she was going to be invited to have sex as I could perceive from the surroundings of that organization and after she kissed one woman on her naïf look I was answered: 75 pages is all you have? It meant my last book to be sent into Farrar Strauss & Giroux which publishes Wilhelm Reich as well as his opponents.

The extent of human life throughout the rigor mortis

Tue Oct 30, 2012 9:07 am

I have found what is perhaps the solution for the physical extent of human life.
At time of the rigor mortis, physicians must capture this energy, kept her and study her in order to understand this energy.

Vizir (Eduardo Alexandre Pinto)

Childhood

Sun Oct 28, 2012 3:25 am

Children change, they grow with mimetic behavior of adults, they castrate their aura by showing muscles in boys or vanity in girls, the most horrendous crime against childhood.
You should read "Character Analysis" by Wilhelm Reich written in 1949 to understand your own bowels.
I can say that I have never grew up, neither had the time for it. I was always in missions but my childhood glorious momentous took place in Escurquela in 1983, I was so happy that I told myself that I didn´t want to grow. Later I thought and found the cliff up above from our yellow house "seen from the window, seen it but being touched by it" that it was my wish to become a writer. I have refused a great poetical love, my artic flower from Aveiro, Bárbara in the name of humankind.
Why I don´t go into Germany for the children rights commune? Because I know too well that project and all my work done in this country is done, so I think but and alike Wittgenstein thought that all philosophical problems or human problems were solved but no, they are infinite as our souls and perhaps freedom. It is our responsibility to carry the torch from our innovated/creative and human scent with a frank opening of our

emotions.

Troubles with money in these times of our age are hard, any one should think for a minute over the emotional hate of the social plague bases on humans as you can perceive how ants work, how birds are free, how cats are independent, how dogs are loyal, how owls are vigilant, how panthers are wild and my plant has 22 years and it is an Anturium.

I was fired because I gave full joy into children

Sun Oct 21, 2012 5:05 am

Back in 1999, I had a job with children, I was told to clean their poo and pee; what it took place was a great reception from the children which I have had embraced with joy. I was immediately fired...

Cancer and Social Emulation

Thu Oct 18, 2012 2:08 am

While people were having parties on their empty honesty, I was working, this applies into the people which think money is food but not emotions, this insecurity on each individual among the actual world, leads into the isolation of many good-hearted people which work their mind with many elements of devotion in the realm of moral beauty. Drinkers and all tomorrow parties belong into the vacuum cleaner; my cancer patient from upstairs knows it too well but she refuses to attend health in the name of social emulation.

Saharasia

Wed Oct 17, 2012 2:47 pm

Religion is about logistic either in private sects like scientology or the terror from the Muslim. The work made by James DeMeo, Saharasia according to my view is not controversial but since the author could trace the origins of violence and oppression as he states in his book but somehow Wilhelm Reich had already found those on his work and DeMeo attacks the Muslim, therefore religion should be abolished. Since religion continues to be the masses opium with more new models of addiction, religion will attract new contracts. Quoting Dr. Reich, prevention is necessary and Dr. Meo is doing a good work since 1978.

Dear love

Justify this son

The Earth and the moon

Yours so soon

From this word

Till June

Shelley

Thu Jul 05, 2012 10:20 am

Shelley was one of the brightest and best, coupling a giant intellect with a highly emotional and impetuous nature. He was always a champion of liberty, but was largely ignored when he tried to promote political and social reform. He was wise enough, however, to realize that his efforts were ineffective, and he chose instead, not to attempt to reshape society, but to transform the individual, to inspire his readers to a greater love of beauty, of nature, and especially of each other. To this end, he poured forth a profusion of gorgeous verse overflowing with brilliant imagery, all aimed at uplifting the good and the beautiful, the free and the loving, while denouncing the social forces that tended to suppress them.
Unfortunately, it was Shelley's fate to be misunderstood by the people of his own time. He was vilified as an evil influence, a free thinker and free lover whose ideas should be abhorred. He pictured himself in his poetic tribute to Keats, "Adonais," as an outcast or a martyr, a "phantom among

men, companionless," bearing a brand upon his brow like that of Cain or of Christ. His life was unorthodox, but his nature was highly sympathetic and filled with devotion to those who were ground down by life and the pressures of a callous society. Perhaps the greatest testimonial was paid to him in letters written by Lord Byron (who, incidentally, disagreed with his political ideas): "...he is, to my knowledge, the least selfish and the mildest of men--a man who has made more sacrifices of his fortune and feelings for others than any I ever heard of." "Shelley...was, without exception, the best and least selfish man I ever knew. I never knew one who was not a beast in comparison."

A universe with no fear it is mature

Thu Jun 28, 2012 7:08 pm

A universe with no fear it is mature. Where this Universe exists in the shape of societies it is what I expect from the work in here because if there is a true relation between sexuality and courage and only for the ones which came to sneak our society feel curious about this aspect. Why are they interested in this, it is related with immortality, often spoked about in words, in this case, it is a mature society, maybe because they had found themselves young and something that is so refreshing that their brand world exists far and wide and in peace.

Writing as therapy

Tue Jun 26, 2012 5:19 pm

Hello,

I had a beautiful childhood, many people and animals were part of my life, many passed away. I am facing a world where the beauty is most of the times hidden in materialism, vanity, selfishness, envy.
I try my best to maintain the levels of justice as if I would be a leaf in the meadow, standing in calm with the attention of someone in care for love. The draw you show is moving, I want to present my gratitude to you

60

because it has triggered my inner child which is always with me, hope that with you too.

We could play in a room with paper and colors, a ping pong ball and a window into the selected poems of joy.

Thank you,

Alex

Joie de vivre

Sat Jun 23, 2012 6:49 pm

A tribute to Mr. José Rodrigues a kind man which had the vision of the modern decay and he withdraw from the world and found refugee somewhere.

My analysis on Paulino Vieira is as it follows: Paulino had a severe education at ´Salesianos College´, he believes that his music comes from God. He his one true child of nature, generous and unique. His smile taken as eccentric is perhaps a nervous reaction that he feels inside his misrepresentation as a person: let us imagine a waiter watching his cd and having nothing to say while the musician worked all his life and the same situation happened with my father, being attacked by a stupid dog on which I kicked with my foot. So Paulino believes that discipline is one essential element into creation, sometimes he loses his patience other times he is very calm. He lives somewhere in Cape Verde. He was arrested and put in a mental prison. Luckily, he plays each year at Cidade da Praia in his country.

My writer eyes have seen the tales of love and glory, dear Lori. Did you know that one good man called Comanche used to help American farmers? There is one story about a father and his daughter; Comanche worked on the farm and shot three mean men.

In Paris, I smoked in honor of my beloved, I could see one beautiful woman (pause for a thought). You know Lori; I was not in Warsaw because I felt I should not go, I was awake all night.

At last I got rid of the German man. Dear Lori, you know that I have travelled all the world in body and in mind, there is no such things as truth and justice; I will seek again and again. It happened that I was traced in time, now while I seek for a young pupil and a girlfriend, I will wait for the life from the Out Space. I am interested in it. My emotions run wild dear Lori, because I have never had time to grow. I was saving lives for about 39 years. I found what it can be the secret of immortality.

Emily Dickinson was right.

I gave my contributions into the sexual revolution which could take place in Germany. I was not understood on this matter.

In America, no one has the courage to reply into my articles.

I have witnesses about Orgon energy in Santo António da Caparica. As well in the quarter of Rêgo in Lisbon.

There was a man who was disciple of Agostinho da Silva, he was a good man, and he carried a bottle of water and an old newspaper. There was a woman with a baby which showed him into the air.

I asked one German how he does not like mirrors and he was fed up. Wilhelm Reich paid a high price sustain the life energy. All my questions were posed into the world, now I want to have a quiet life.

Oh I dreamed about the dim

There were people like Giselle.

I thought on the realm of him

And all it started like ´elle´.

I dreamed about the dim yes and it tasted like a journey into the morning, I had a brainstorm and someone disturb me.

Everything was saved with effort even if I could not reflect about poetry in Lisbon.

The population was said to say that they have to go on their way and the attack was on my person. It means that somehow I cannot carry the world on my shoulders, though it seems that I was induced with this mission alike Sisyphus.

Somehow, I could not predict on what the world seems to attend as games when me, Keith and Fritz were on the road talking about Eric Barnes.

I sat to say what can I does it have me big black and blue, the kids of Galicia. I think I am looking for new shapes of societies. It is bombastic this emotion. I have the distinct feeling that all means a direction into the energy of children because the world can be positive yes but we have to make from character the same positive energy with ´locke´ features upon him.

After Fonsagrada I slept near some pines and an owl awoke. It is a smart bird. Like writers they work day and night. It took one year to understand that we have to be stupid.

Professor Noam Chomsky is right; he told me 'I wish I could share your optimism'. Just because I felt happy through music I thought he could the same but he does not believe that it is possible.

I wanted to feel an orgasm extended into saudade.

Subliminal intelligence means to develop a bridge from people. The stones are visible at one side of the mirror which is the skies that expand into the realm of a thousand spirits awakened by a soul seeker around freedom. On the course of history, history herself cannot undertake into the conscious to carry the supreme moment of love.

I dreamed about a lake, thought of Mr. Delfim, everything was vanished from Earth. The reality of our days is the totus tus based on emptiness, far from being one good reason to attend moral which was extinguished from the natural understanding of humans. Now that the shit is away, at least some humble people could talk about their lives. Sadness is everywhere it is just disguised by plastic surgery on the realm of allegories which mean a way to deny into the population the access in the wealth we all need. Part of my endless job as poet is to inspire but and again stupidity there is nothing and that no one can do. People on the 21th century are complete idiots and one aspect which I could attend is for example the social control by different sources of the emotional plague and I wonder where the natural love is.

In my country is forbidden to have a brainstorm or to scream.... I could bring Orgonon into here where the emotional cowardice appeared like automatic people. Now a little white cat has passed. I miss my blonde drummer which had long hair and later he cut because I also did it. The bandits are free, courts are closed at Sundays for example (here I point New York as the worst example on Earth in analogy into the Jesus and Mary Chain which had given a good result on music but both failed to understand the emotional honesty of societies). One other example is the relation of justice and well fair. One other example is how snow can trigger good feelings around the body. Miss Henderson is somehow honest because she answers the phone with good morning how can I help you. Professor Chomsky told me that am not possible to tell the truth so I stopped. While Stephen Hawking needs time to understand women even with so many difficulties he has to endure to explain his theories about the cosmos.

I brought Tapados into my place, the dim near a chestnut where Bárbara has a beautiful garden. Now is sun which mean love comes along. I wonder what my father as saw in Mozambique.

I am well just doing not want to mix with the sick crowd. I left bread on the balcony from the place where I am. Young adults are laughing and oh I thought about the world´s commitment with the ideas around religion and other facts.

Once I met a boy to whom I taught him some English words.

A long time which I don´t dance, Olga was a good dancer. Pororoca is a disco in Belém do Pará, the word means the confluence of salted waters with ocean waters.

What I have learned is that the poet condition is a dance made of good things and alike Victor Peter does with his walks. I miss the American Christian girl.

The feeling of oppression is often a social tool like discos and so on. It is possible to communicate without words.

It happens that the child in me is tense because it cries every time it thinks on something which is far but it is concrete.

I dreamed about Miguel Ângelo he was finishing a book from me with his way of drawing so particular like a noble shape from his hands.

I dreamed about a number which its last three numbers were 528. Once I won 600€ with the number. I did not give up in the studies, I pray into God and he guides me, I have my own way of travelling and I think of my friend which is blind and aged around 80´s (people tend to seduce her to steal her money). I saw so many men being robbed by Brazilian women for example. In fact, I saw my father being annoyed by a stupid dog after giving all to Portugal. Today some white men were screaming, I was asking myself why did they not screamed Salazar, of course they were not brave enough and they went away.

Apartment life is boring, I remember about a man and a donkey; they were passing in the center of Portugal and slept on our house. Magic times. It is somehow a lesson for those which cannot tolerate nature. There are few people who still dream and work hard on the domain of freedom and respect. After some time, it came into my mind that the beauty hides what nature shows and that is the heart of the dense white matter of everything.

It´s cold. One girl from Lapa wrote me that she felt the cold. By the kitchen in Tapados on the outside I was seated with one more baby attending the energy from the future. So much earlier, one woman shown his baby into the skies, it was a moving moment in Campolide, Lisbon.

I could see one mother giving 2€ to her son and the child was happy. I gave all my possessions I have nothing like Alla Sazonchik my good Russian friend.

I was told that one woman cried so much that blood came from her eyes.

One couple was so much in love; they sell flowers into the people inside cars who were passing, such a beautiful image of love, tremendous moment of magic.

The wind came along from a distant land; in my awake I could understand how I inspired thousands of Germans in the spring of 2008.

Some women passed wishing a good time into the world. I appreciate their good will.

I found out why human thought is being operated. It will take some time to describe it.

The diva which was at the mountains of Lordelo impressed Filipe the cousin of my cousin Jorge Miranda; he looked at her with astonished eyes. Filipe used to wear a crucifix and often he played with me.

Human thought could live under the banner of poetry, in fact poet's day it always stands in the first day of Spring which means that is a sign of hope, the task to endure now is to hold on while the people which do not wear sensible ears as poets have is to understand the moral of these days. It is somehow a massive shape of ups and downs on which emotions have an important role as it concerns these people. My task on this domain has been done.

It is a fact that doctors work hard and that getting home and to watch the news well I would advise them to do not matter so much because if there is moral on them no frustration can be felt.

There was a girl called Vera on my elementary school, I used to see her at the entrance of the big wooden door and she smiled openly. Paulo Costa was a boy which did not know how to play football.

I could quote one of my sentences in order to cooperate with the immanent logic upon this book and that is: a penniless logic does not disdain from something.

Something could be for example a disdain for people which are extreme sensitive, then comes at the surface in the relation a kind of one more disdain. There is something warm about the rain, it is being said, I know it is true, I could experience it. I also know that I will be understood.

From Estoril I was going in a crowded train back home, sneaking the place where I could see the trails alike I used to do it on the subway of Lisbon which had nice red carriages.

It took me 26 years to center Orgon energy; I call it God that is all.

There was a postcard from Alex which could save the Rainforest; it is on my room at Santo António da Caparica while here there is a real paper wall from a man who dedicated him into the people which cannot give up even if their wings were hounded on the journey. I guess that is why people give up, so the importance of poetry and philosophy in these twisted times. As well as science. I think we must not give so much attention into politicians.

I awoke with the feeling of my soul being universal. After passing through the 'saudosistas', the 'sensacionistas' I met Urbano Tavares Rodrigues, a kind man full of wisdom.

I tend to think on the spell of flower so intense and gorgeous like the good angel which drove my thoughts into the realm of love for 3 decades.

A new logic is always like a poem it tolerates the deafness of the ages and that is why poetry is healthy.

A long murmur whistles, it is long and new like the appeal from poetry on the way to one other call, the one from the roving tale of a Polish myth. The sunset has intense features, I miss the sunset. From here I cannot see him and I recall the circus Nómada which stayed near me and I could hear the voice of a friend in time, it was the Spiderman, the boy which lost his scholar degree due to the readings of Spiderman. He could recognize me in time against all odds.

Even if I had found God (Orgon), I have to bear with its importance and find refugee. I want peace.

In my country is forbidden to think, I know that I am right, just can't cope with the dilemma from the work on which I made into most of my students and the fact that they failed but with at least one good result coming from Germany I am happy because I can rely on his energy.

I have hidden many things from people, sadly most of them could not tell me, and they wanted to talk (most of them, not all).

There is good woman called Fernanda in Lordelo, she knows well about faith.

I have hidden many things from people because they would not be ready for them.

Fernanda (Fénix) for example is one good woman who did it all well with me and my poem into her meant my love for her, deep in the Lisbon night.

We were in love for about 24 hours, we kissed, walked together, we were happy and free in the summer of 1987. The seagulls know about this love energy.

I dreamed about my muse Lígia, we played and laughed in full joy.

The rain will come perhaps. People in here never saw someone working at full speed of thought.

I had prayed into God in order to guide people on their task on each journey, I could hear children and the church bells. The eclipse is not forced away, there is love somewhere I know it.

In here I tend to think about lobotomists and politicians, I better forget them because it is sick.

In Dusseldorf, I played football for a bit in the middle of the crowd and I found happiness in the middle of so much stress.

My book about Portugiesisch Literature in German was read in the big room at Kirchdorf where the night was tender.

I remember to attend Crisfal College and meeting there the twins Castro who were marathon runners.

Tonight, I met two boys which were passing with music on their hands. My neighbor was playing perhaps a saxophone. A stupid dog barked at me and a stranger went into the third floor of this building. I collected one stone from the sidewalk and came home because it was getting cold and I feel that somehow I inspired people in some way on which I have felt.

The articles which were published have around 500 readers each one so I am pleased because I can guide someone in this world even from this tiny place.

I remember to be at the Caixa das Indústrias placed in Areeiro where somewhere down at the basement there was a supermarket and from the window of my mother's office I could see so many things while she could see me playing at my elementary school where at the age of 7 I was already a veteran in football.

I made love at open air all over Europe also very close from this house at Gulbenkian garden with my first catholic girlfriend.

I dreamed about Mr. Carlos Celso and Mr. Delfim who were together near the end of Rua de Campolide.

Miss Francisca was my catholic teacher at the Santo António de Campolide church, she was kind. We used to be at the top of a tower to learn about the words of Jesus.

I dreamed about a good world, it was intense and beautiful.

Children passed with joy, believing on the things their eyes meet each time they sing aloud, their perception of thing is pure, and they must know the words of the good.

Poem into the sagacity

Tenderness keeps the innocent in calm
You can enter around my dreams and attend beauty
It is all colored and peaceful

Look at the owl, he has new eyes and it sings
Alike the merchant from Greifswald which took care of my eyes
Dare dear horizon, to attend the dancing area of stars
Up in Saturn, there are many moons
The city moved so again I stopped
Then the realm of a consensual thought
Moved in order to shine for all logic
Then it calms and it is the poem himself.

I saw the portrait of a woman lying on a comfortable bed, she is naked and she reads the stars with the infusion of a logic which derives from the unknown, in this case, her and me, we dive into this picture and yes, we make love like Eve Libertine and Adam Jankowiak on the Glamour Hotel in Poznan. While the feature of any measure of the taste suiting on the examples history has shown from the dilemmas all over the sample steps of each virgin prune over the table of calm. This is why I used to walk in Sintra, to make love there and to attend children's sexuality with the beauty of the hour when singers spread out their poetry and all lessons are love lessons. Somewhere where the rainbow was double with Miss Sílvia Cardoso and her tender virginity that our volley matches meant to be our Austrian answer into Nani Moretti in 1995. So every little portion of the sick societies where a refined Indian in Brazil can at least on his best, attend beauty from his freedom that no one can interfere, the best lesson of wild life in its pure shape of freedom.

The direction of society is between family and unity from all humans. Nature teach us to have ears and eyes as well the sense of strategy, cannot predict on how these lines can produce a good future into the vivid reality of the unity which reigns on the universe, it is then another example of how to handle with the mentioned logic upon the great sequences of thought. As it concerns the body, we in Earth as our country, need to spread sexuality in all cultures because it is one natural element of devotion and a kind approach into the warmth. When Dr. Alexander Lowen refers to spirituality on his teachings he means the existing shapes of thought among culture, as example of ways through the days. They should be days of open hand.

One example of freedom is being taught since there is music, music teaches how to embrace freedom and we do not need to run to achieve freedom like most of the people do because they are afraid of contact, of course there are good exceptions like the moving people coming to the realm of the simple but at the same time deep things among the days.

Poetry also guides as well as prays because we are all parts of this unity conferred by God. Streets are filled with hope and even if some of the new things came to sneak with mirrors, the anger of my good looks buys a little portion of the word man which loves a word woman somewhere where there is a heaven above with a rising moon and many of the good dancers of the snow information provided by a good and protecting Yeti. These were the thoughts of my magical mystery tour between an elegant look over them.

I can only decadence, all moral values are finished.

I have three women friends who are poetesses and one male friend who is a poet, all of them are refined people and I follow them with care. Lost contact with one male Portuguese poet called Alexandre Crespo and almost forgot about the Spanish poet from Galicia.

I have good relations with the Turkish; they are warm people as well with Muslims and Jews.

Frisian and the Occitan idioms are one solution but not all at its full length.

Many alcoholic people asked me for advice and all they want is to be felt on the inside.

The stress from the unknown makes from a good person the angriest one because some of others spell badly the name of love and I can show from one point at a specific place where it lays the fair icon of justice, the examples exist worldwide and I am lucky to know them by heart.

The snake's skin up over the land were brown, these snakes liked this land. I remember the eagle which lived on Santo António da Caparica on the cliff where I pushed the rain with my mind.

For some decades, original music doesn't appear, I can trace it on the late 80's.

There are good humans, just don't know where are they, I could see them in many different places, and we are all looking for some brightness among the iron curtain of the emotional hate between humans. Once again, the animal kingdom, the vegetal kingdom, the mineral kingdom is paying a heavy price for all the hate that is taking place.

I am looking for my own kind. As the eagle where she carefully patrols the skies with high commands in tribute to all great warriors like Geronimo. I am an Indian, proudly blessed by the hands of God (I must hide some facts); my own Gondal is my free heat over the ages of the uprising of the clock work and its speed. Things over here cannot share any optimism with young believers and alike Fred Astaire, we dance and a doctor complies to speak about papers, which drinks poetry in these days? The boys which I met in Amsterdam, the marines, the bums, the poor and the blind, for God sake, how much more imprisonment must the human race carry on, can I ask, of course and it is a flying horse as magic kingdom with emperor clothes and the beat of many portions of hope even with the beginning of love, sexuality, the cosmos and beyond what is unseen.

I could enter in the realms of Nuno Travanca, a poet who lived with his mother. He gave me once 5€ for me to go on hospital. We used to chat often on 'Canal Poesia' at the IRC Network.

I could see one girl at the subway with a green book, something happened between both, later I saw her in Rossio with the same book.

Fernanda used to make up and I met her in Restauradores, she was wearing a dark long skirt, I was astonished for the fact, nevertheless good days.

The good people from Santo António da Caparica on which between 1991 and 1994 I was among and where I was loved.

Sinead O'Connor made a beautiful song called 'The Emperor's New Clothes', she is a good woman, and she needs support. I think Pope John Paul the Second made a pray into her.

Rui Cerveira was a teacher of Karate Do for many years at Judo Clube de Portugal in Rua Dom Carlos Mascarenhas.

I used to like of one girl down at Rua Marquês de Fronteira at a yellow building, she was Sandra, a blonde girl on which we walked into the high school together so close under her umbrella.

My vision of life it is an idealistic nature.

I used to think for endless hours, my father found for us a beautiful house in the quarter of Campolide, a fresh area coming from the Monsanto Forest. My room is very interesting, it has white curtains made by my mother, a desk where I used to study, a single bed, toys, a television. From there I could listen into the trains of the railway station, the ships from the river Tagus, cat's society, seagulls and the deep blue sky across my childhood imagination already being an ideal.

In 1978, me and my father were at the Lisbon harbor where we talked with an American that was on a submarine, I told into the American: 'Captain!' and he smiled.

The first word in German idiom was feuer.

The first word in Russian was ja tibia lu blu.

I and Pedro Verde at the elementary school was good friend though I was the first to learn how to read. I used to hold the class door and look at Pedro.

Later I had a girlfriend called Ana Verde, we had sex in the living room of her house for one hour and she was exhausted, she thought I made tantric sex. I simply had practiced how to hold on my premature ejaculation and could make many girls happy with sex.

Love exists yes, nowadays is related with economy as well as with natural selection thinking posture. The Darwin concept of life and nature is wrong because some many millions of people are exiting with their intelligent structures like it does and behaves my favorite muse Patrícia Guerreiro.

Incest is legal in Portugal.

Magda is one refined woman from whom I was in love. She had long dark hair. Hope she is well.

At the age of 15 I predicted that I would have not any children and that proved to be right.

My Anturium is well; the root has 22 years in my hands.

My bible was offered by my grand-mother in 1982.

Yesterday has rained in São Paulo, Mafalda Nascimento is there, she a good student. She seeks love and she will find, she is elegant.

In 1989 a couple visited us at Seladinho, they were living close to our house.

I spent one year training at Ginásio Clube Português which is located near a refined square where there is a beautiful garden. My ping pong teacher took me and two other colleagues into somewhere in a white Renault 4; later I met Canina there at the football field. I have met two Canina´s. Canina means a boy which is short in analogy into dogs. The first Canina scored a good goal at my elementary school while the second was trapped in our high school though he could have fought back and around 1995 he found many girlfriends, I used to see him at Rua Marquês de Fronteira where many social cartoons were placed at the prison was. I have visited this prison in 1988; I was attending the van from the António Coelho Dias printing services.

I had a post card from Patrícia Guerreiro in the year 2000, where she recognizes Isabel and me as a brave writer. She is well, my best student!

I have met the chaplain of the Hospital Curry Cabral: in the year of 1988 I have visited the chapel of São José Hospital where I was working.

Ponette was a young woman which I met near Saldanha in the year of 1999 when I was dating my Lolita.

I do not understand why leute use cars, Yves is one good man, I hope he is well, met him in the year of 1989 at the La Loire valley and oh how I remember the beautiful girl who was a roadie into a French band. She was in dark: in those times, girls were interesting. Du bist geil Ana

Margarida I?

Artur da Gama was the step son of Vasco da Gama. There were many cigars and cigarettes at the center of Przezmierowo where I used to go either by bike, by foot or by car. My maneuvers were firm as the lifetime service into the dear Lord alike Jane Eyre and her husband somewhere where there were Gytrash. She is one wise woman like Zofia Dambek used to tell me when she had length me some books. A good student on wisdom affairs. It is almost one element of curiosity when she saw the sexual activity of insects at her garden. I used to see snails near the pavement. There were funny traffic signals near the forest. I used to enter the forest by one side close to the shop of one man who used to live at Ul. Ogrodowa, 99 Przezmierowo, Poznan, Poland and in great style I drove into the wild but good nature of the environment of Poland.

Pascoal is one good man, he is strong and he and Paulino Vieira recorded some songs in Portuguese.

Eusébio is well known in Poland, one man remembers the matches from the Black Panther from SL Benfica. He comes from the land of elephants. He has his own way of fighting.

My father is well, thank you.

I wonder how the good people from Poland are.

Dulcet Pontes is one good singer, I saw her at the Belém Park in1997 when I have won a match. Can time forgive humans, I hope that time teaches the young generations like all of them and I should know that the most intense journey is into the future.

Box 481 is one elegant woman which had given me food in the mid of the Millennium.

Carla was a dog which was my friend, I used to give her good cheese and she smiled while moving her toe.

The cycle of life is made of a season in the realm of achieving dignity, I know it by experience and that the humble perceive existence with refined conditions.

Pedro Mantorras gave one champions cup into SL Benfica, later he was forgotten and abandoned. He is one good man.

The mystery of existence is one aspect of the expansion-tension laws of the cosmic nature and that means that we make things here on the Universe with the conscious of a certain meaning which picks the force of the sober timeless distinctions.

In addition to the green eyes under the vision which bubbles and it peruses all my students, I feel great gratification and inside me, a feeling of rebirth like a slow motion in perpetual replay of the deepest multi identity on which I could feel like an experience as a poet.

As a writer I often find out in the streets the vivid realm of the languor on each dream as fulfillment of being part of any one´s way of being inside existence from the direction which derives from all the processes over and over time as if time would be a passing present. The prayers of many deep natural philosophers somewhere in Medina where the boys sing like the beautiful women of their nature of being a free heat is a part of the sense of diving on the sweetest caress which feeds the heart. This is my assumption as the answer into all the Darwinists.

In 1982, I collected money on a blue circular box into the Portuguese Institute of Rheumatology. Not so far from here, there is one bridge where children walked about one week ago, they were happy and their teacher told them out loud, ´some good strength on those legs!´.

One feeling from my office at Santo António de Caparica was to perceive things as Sempiternal baptisms of eternity, while the battle takes time on my discoveries and among the other things which were a mock on the sandy winds of the Tamarack and many different ways of being idiotic, like the treats which I was living for a period of 7 months.

Sadly, the water from Tapados is gone but luckily, I keep no regret over the Darwinists which want to win over strong petals in the trenches, mainly because what is unseen is reachable in the heart of contentment somewhere here or in Dax.

I felt eternity and one day on my personal freedom where Bruno Ganz took time to set beauty over the sensation of being an angel, here where the sweet child of Paprika. Paprika was one shy boy with spots on his face; he was virgin when I met him. Paprika is one shop at Rua Sampaio Pina, from the daughter of one plumber. The sister of Pedro Barata is red and I was the first boy at high school to have beard. My father has white beard while Paulino Vieira has white curls on his hair. They had taken his hair, police that was. Alexander the painter, is one good man, he was very polite when he told me that he had to go into Berlin to exhibit his pieces of work. Nossa Senhora de Fátima is on the house of Dr. Maria Demeser. Many religious figures stand on this country as well in Portugal.

How Elisa from Lordelo/Vila Real could be a waiter on the house of my neighbors in Rua General Taborda I was not told, she somehow was the lover of my grand-father.

I remember well the days of Chiado; it took me two intense years to find students. I have worked 24 hours a day. One man asked me that. As well as a lawyer in Jeeser with his bodyguard. One man with his bodyguard in Santo António de Caparica looked scary but when I placed him on my eyes he become emotional and lost his stiffness.

A joke from 23 years stands among the eyes of Anne of Greifswald. A tribute into Mr. Dr. Flora Bento which gave me a cigar in the year of 1999. The morality of mankind leads free-thinkers to feel the world as a place not as a random place and that is what Alex Constantine is doing.

I learned that leute do not seek for help, they hide their needs, most of the times, and somebody has to run in order to help them.

There is an evidence of morality where leute are and that lasts for about 10 000 years, according to Dr. Wilhelm Reich.

If one Christian faith belongs into the world, why so many defenses on this moral realm? It is my belief that the circular thread of birds around the healing nature which revamps existence has much logic alike the work of the wild cat that came to shout in the street.

I remember of my music teacher which was at the bus, she has followed my steps, I was 10.

My second music teacher was much more severe.

My guitar teacher was a gentleman while my drums teacher was a junky. I liked them both nevertheless.

I remember to have visited one meeting of the catholic radio of Portugal. Many leute were there. Leo knows well what is leute.

Miguel Dray was my colleagues at Ginásio do Alto do Pina. His sister Rita Dray stood from the top of the high school stairs and looked at me, she was pretty, and everybody looked at us.

The friend of Mr. Dray was Rui who had a coffee place at the Bus station from the old Rodoviária Nacional from which on the year of 1989 I made hundreds of journeys, in Avenida Casal Ribeiro. My friend Filipa Albuquerque took some paper money on that street in the year of 1995 or 1996. Bruno a lovely young man was being taken care by my comrade Filipa which many years later got married with a beard guy.

Mr. Amadeu is one refined gentleman known as Pistola, he has worked as a professional on a radar. Some gentleman at Pastorinha are interesting, the last time I was there, one man said he liked to be President of the United Nations.

In Santo António de Caparica, Mr. Pires is one calm man which often pays into children ice cream in order for them to attend joy. (Joy was the dog of Rui and Paulo.)

Dona Elizete is one divine woman from Santo António da Caparica; she has learnt many things from me. She is well I suppose.

She sounds as she spells, I would tend to know her by heart and it was a kind care for her way of passing through the outcome of beauty within the emulation facts around the girl with sensible shoes who would crash the harbor with some of what is the realm of joy.

It counts as if when one or twenty kisses would be a refined blesses from the mixture of many dives upon the proper ´mélange´ and alike Mário the father of Sara Ferreira probably the author of the sentence: ´Avô Cantigas ao Poder´ which means Grand Pa the Singer into Power.

I would dare to say that the world is somehow under the banner of something logic as the measures of love which are always a tension based on the worry for the kind care on which my peer people are existing. For example, one good friend from Linda-A-Velha knows well how she could turn wealth as a magic powder on her realm of magic. She is my best example on how things can change.

How is it going, my fur is somehow huge now.

It is a sunshine day in here.

For the many women are broken hearted.

A wind which flies as the thaw on how

The clear sacred shattered bathed screams to perform beauty.

And it is bliss born from a liquid fist

Those who fought to twist upon the land of some other portmanteau of doubt, brings the music up in a leather alike a melody being sang from the tank where the wise gather their power to induce the wind in solid and free forms of energy. One reason why the minerals are one portion of time lays on the fact that the rotation from an afternoon walk, a breeze coming from the days where hands were open and the longing fate was a magical reason based on the same liquid being wind, from them all into the love motion because we were talking for endless hours about the water and sand, the we took a shower together.

There are boys and girls which are fragile alike me, they tend to seek comfort on animals, they are fine people, it is my creed speaking. As for me I am one child of nature, nature is a high commander of the Earth matters.

As it matters on the realm of thought, one man called Phil Collins gave up playing music while Cher gave up as well.

I found that the people have many tricks to cope with the Darwin thing which is one domain on which I tend to keep distance because it does not comply into the love relation upon humans. It is my conviction that it can be applied into the all other three kingdoms.

Work is energy in movement, a notion of physics. The domains of biology, chemistry, for example, these three fields of knowledge are a helping hand into the understanding of the natural laws of all the things which matter the realm of the human body as well on the other three kingdoms. Nutrition is one evidence on the attention on which these kingdoms need to have the tonality of wealth. It takes time to understand why some names mean something, for example: if one person called Lori, has many qualities on her or one person called Alfred, this means that all the memory requires what it does not hurt and to make it conscious is the process of attending calm.

One address on which I used to write still exists: Rua dos Sapateiros, 91-3º 1100-596 Lisboa.

One other address is Rua Diogo de Couto, 13-2ºEsq, 2795 Linda-A-Velha. One street, from which taxi drivers find it hard to find, is Rua Escoura in Braga.

My uncle José Miranda lives on Rua Teófilo Braga and he has an interesting place.

I was shocked when I have arrived into Santo António and saw the automatic people up and down every block; a feeling of a certain distance led me to stay indoors where I can be my Unic (Um Adeus Regular).

For 12 years now that I smoke and the scope of poetry goes where loving goes on each parcel of hate where the logic of the trenches does not disdain from the old logic of being and again emerged from the parade style of many of the memories on which the words live with. It is certain that the world can live with sounds like birds do and they fly like a wonder, so high and active as if a painter could love one farmer woman on the mountain where a cow feeds the couple with many years ahead.

Why did the sexual revolution fail on the 21th century? Because the world was not ready, there were some good signs about this but it was misunderstood by some people who could trigger this energy predicted in 1930 by Dr. Wilhelm Reich. It happened in San Francisco in the mid 60´s of the 20th century. Now San Francisco it is a city more open into a good ecological environment, maybe a possible way for the love energy to come out in an organized way like Dr. Elfsworth Baker thought about this matter socially speaking.

Bô ta fixe is a word which means detachment from being sad, it means that what the Google translator cannot introduce, to be well.

Some local bandits were all the time in hell, the usual service at every place where rioters have always been existing like cheap bananas (chorona), there are two other kinds in Brazil, prata and pacovã.

I worry about Sara Ferreira because from what I know, she used a bypass at the age of 12 and taking Risperdal, so young while the father has to work hard to support his family.

I also worry about Daniela Ferreira, my cousin who finds herself blocked by the contrast of her high sensibility towards a muscular world where she has to live, in that region the tendency is to have a couple relations and it is everywhere.

Filipa do Carmo and me we used to make love like fools on her tiny room near my high school where Cicely was born. Cicely is one character of one of my essays. Cici was the girl which looked me when I sang one tune from Ramones in our little coin d´amour at our high school. We were determined my generation and freedom existed for a period of about 20 years in Portugal, and then it was finished. Yes, people swallow shit and it hurts to see the traitors being everywhere. Fortunately, many of us survived and are in close contact.

The Polish priest on whom I had a conversation was kind, a little shy, we spoke in French.

The words typed in a typing machine in an azert keyboard were my company during my childhood. Many works were made there. I worked with several types of typing machines.

The world does not accept poets, what can I do? Nothing but to wait. It is sad.

I remember when I was at the Alfa Cinema, met there the Portuguese singer, Lena D´Água, I was around 10 years of age.

In Koln, children were mean as well as the people from the train on my way into other stupid person, after having made psychoanalysis for two hours and that was the reward after two years of hard work. In here the structure is the same, then bad mood comes fast like a cannonball on the way to the next random thought, made of marble made of stone. I wish I was far away from this place because it really it brings nothing than crucial times when I should be doing what I am doing exception goes for the love felt with the woman in dark trousers and the sun on which I took for brief minutes. This is the world dear reader. Paulino Vieira could taste this at Campolide. The exact exchange appears like muddy waters made of alcohol inside the bowels of the structure where no one accepts poetry, so it takes plenty of time and patience to attend this effect of emotional deafness, even if the people laugh or scorn about something absurd which is their lives.

Alla Sazonchik the Russian brought Nietzsche into her place at the area of Bahamas, Princetown that is. She gave all her books, then she had the hope to find calm there but she found a hard time there, now she has a brain damage.

Alla from Estonia likes a Spaniard, she has one beautiful soul though she cheated when she has shown her pictures from Maarja, then she gave up and found a hard way into herself.

Madame Loreta Rimkute likes to walk.

I think that the world problem, talking about Darwin is about something which I must repeat for endless times, about the lack of love existing in our societies since about some decades. I have never experienced love again no matter how hard I try to find him. I could go somewhere but it is my conviction from experience that is no longer possible (maybe I am wrong...). But I have a feeling that I am right.

The fragglers are one good society, they knew well how to produce an outsider shape of independence born from their working spirit like ants do and alike young Americans do nowadays.

The pots of my great grand-mother have produced refined and natural food, I remember to pee outside and how the liquid was so strong. She used to kindle the fire with some mixture of a bluish color.

It is said to say that from this night where my mental orgasm could enhance the appearance of the decal of my purity as vulture of one late night figure which was the showcase of a similar shadow, a below form somewhere in the side walking alike when I was reading Castor at Santo António da Caparica.

One senior woman was surprised 'that she still could be surprised...' and I think of her with compassion as well as in the child on which the father showed her my figure when I was passing on the way to a place called 'Avinhão'. In this place, I met Hermínia Silva with her friend, in the mid 90´s. I saw one Portuguese actress called Beatriz Costa in downtown coming out of her hotel in a sportive car, somewhere around the 90´s as I have found her in Sevilla in 1982 or 1983 at Hotel Don Paco.

8:48 am and 5:57 am are two time dates which had accompanied during many years. 1:12 was also one-time date but from The Netherlands from a man which worked for cinema as producer of explosives. I live now with a sick mother, completely insane, the vision of her but was awful. I remember the feet kick of the guitar player of one English band called Fine Young Cannibals at the San Remo Festival into the TV presenter (why should I care about sick mother´s if the bird sings so well now?). Since my early morning he sings, I have counted two, the former was much more powerful.

American youth have everything except the good appeal on something concrete like what farmers did, so they are locked inside apartments like me, well I took this decision because people from this quarter are mean. Maybe in October things will be better.

I dreamed about Paula, when we waved goodbye, she was in blue; her eyes meant something for me.

Aunt Junia is one sensible woman with great devotion with his husband which died in 2009 when I was making correspondence with my Polish fiancée.

I dreamed about a Brazilian woman with sexy underwear.

One man had played in Lamego football team and has a Portuguese wife. I there you here, oh the things which lift our dreams!

As vast and radiant as the curled hair around the days of a thousand sunny graces, they came from the skies, I must protect my kind clouds in order to prevent more escape from poetry. Poetry lies with me initially as something open into the erogenous sober temper of the desire on and on over a cherish tree, love was and is immanent into all of this.

The mystery something is perhaps Orgon, people often recall it as something natural which it is, so we have to take care of this energy.

My grand-mother Alice was very active woman, she used to make me a wine juice from the kitchen of our original land. I remember the pipes which were going into the ´quintã´ where the pigs were smelling things all the time. They were pink.

Maybe the phenomenon of emulation which is real has higher forms of meaning.

I remember to see the urinary system with my cousin João. She became a vet and I a writer.

Mónica Sofia has multiple sclerosis, she used to live in a room being under the cares of three women, hired to perform the task while the mother which became lesbian spent the all-day having sex and Mónica could inside this situation write good poems in Portuguese. I was there and was put away from her.

My manual working class teacher lived in Olaias where now it is only sadness all around the area. We have played mini-golf together at the garden of Roma in Lisbon where now it stands a parking place. This area was a good occupation in free forms of playing, mainly youth, all of it was destroyed.

If justice must be induced, then let her come with the necessary elements of all aspects which can establish truth.

God is angry, why in the first-place things are not as fair as they should be?

At times like this there is but one way and that is to attend the calm from a good human when nature is abandoned all around the world. I would say: Jestem tutaj (I am here).

What can the people from do in the course of years in order to establish truth? It takes time and perhaps many threads to awake truth inside the nature of things.

Birds know well the meaning of existence; they adore singing when it comes to a straight talk with people.

António is one friend of mine, he used to use walking sticks, later in time two girls defended me after I looked for the place he liked to be aside a gas station in Costa de Caparica. He spoke Afrikander with me.

Mozart is always one divine company when I endure my task of writing which means to think and vice versa.

Why is my mother insane I do not know?

God has punished the people from here, I awoke and it came a bird.

There is one woman called Dona Maria Teresa, she has Alzheimer. I tend to think that natural selection is and again under the banner of the non-existing love among human or like I wrote economy interferes with this natural condition of nature as it was revealed this afternoon with a huge ´tempête´ in Lisbon. I miss the Spanish doctor who has a house on the other side of this small apartment. Often I was going outside or I was inside talking to old friends, none of them appeared.

One boy sold me an owl doll for 20 cents, he had a watch on his arm and together with one other kid they were collecting money.

It was funny and amusing to see children collecting money at the end of the free market in Stralsund, spring of 2008. Tobias used to look at me when I was smoking.

In one afternoon I used to seat down in front of the São Pedro de Alcântara garden, the light was a mid-previous spring kind, the leafs of the trees were made of an interesting green and often I drank water from the public fountain (perhaps it is finish now). Many things took place on that garden. The last good thing was in April of 2009 when I was walking with my Polish girlfriend, there.

Alike once that is said, a horse was steeping into the sponsored mountain and the great bliss lied on the mental Orgonomic thought based on the military idea of a dismantle of the wooden wall upon the limits of the entrance of the exact curled hair on the way from a giant waterfall.

Andrea Boticelli understood beauty and he sings with a refined quality into the world because it heals and it touches our senses.

Vaclav Havel wrote: ´Letters to Olga´ a good book produced in the prison. I have good memories from Czech Republic.

Cicciolina has promised into the dictators of the world to have sex with them if they would stop their actions. They were executed by Americans.

Mélange is a word which means mixture.

We tend to wake with an emotional atmosphere made of desires and it is one golden example on how poetry must endure the task of tact among the sewing for example.

Poetry heals and its taste feels like the first time we ever saw one good element of truth as in the ascending effect of the allegory of history even if she comes on the page 2000 of some catalog made on the web.

Socially speaking we can endure the task of the great birth from one direction where the actions tend to be something concrete rather than a thousand ideas born from the liquid taste of a yellow portrait taken from a foggy stream among the realm of nature.

The upper part of houses is always a cozy area to attend calm. In areas where the volume of one or more aspects of division of things in the realm of the social organization, it is called for the healing process of the people which need support, a kind of endurance where must learn from their own selfish private concerns as metaphor for what the societies hide in order that the natural organization of nature can revamp forever in the great strains of peace.

So there I am here counting stars and clouds in the process of knowing what is the essence of humans on their inner core and from where they do not want to see and today for example, the rain came to warn people. Only one bird could understand this at least at the place where I am now. No single human could understand this natural structure which guides the natural science of existence (I forgot about a cat, he sneaks and shows his concerns when he passes downstairs).

I was riding into the post office to find books, I found: ´Les Coulisses de l´Anarchie´ by Flor O'Squarr that was in Przezmierowo under a Polish web site with the name allegro.

Pt-Pl is one word game made by the old registration on cars, means the event which took place three years ago where two Capricorns are exhibiting at the center of the Poznan. Bought some regional socks there and tasted a good cheese from the Polish mountains.

I dreamed about a black car in Paris driving wildly. Somehow Lady Diana contacted me.

It is one refined element to feel the intact world upon the songs of the seagulls where the basis of all lampoons is the register of many solutions into the existential questions made from humans.

The four kingdoms do not need to attend the burst of all the waving honey capsules of artificial ´royaumes´, they know well the fads and fashions of each age, their performance is lively loud and clear as the good waterfall of what exists after the infinite.

When I was arriving into Poland in the year of 2009, I could taste the beauty of the land. The first time I was there was in 1995 where I have visited Auschwitz.

Here the repose of an ancient lute, some of the trails left on the modern world of words, some windy spirit complies into the amusing tempo around the souvenir of many shapes of work as a direct answer into the global organization of existence.

It takes time to understand the lifts of the necessary tools to work upon the structure of many good events which some of them lie on the accurate form of the repose of the gratitude inside the logic of calm.

Somehow the things which led me into an anonymous condition are a part of the invisible work I make with people, for their benefit.

We can forgive a lot of things into a genius but not all of them, I have forgiven one of them and let one other to be at its own peace. From both I have learned a lot, still I am supporting them on their legacy. One other which moved into the South of Lisbon and as I can predict has a calm life by teaching Jeet Kune Do.

Finally, I have reached the stage of the wise. It was on the awakening of my nap. I have made some reflections and concluded that the calm I was meant the concilium of my body amidst people. One bird came to eat the bread which I have left on the terrace.

I have found Rocky a young dog which I by morning usually caress with my hands.

When I was reading Letters to Olga by Vaclav Havel, I could feel the socio-economic aspects of the Portuguese.

Rocky came with one teenager and I asked her if she was daughter of the woman which at every morning walks Rocky, she was confused and could not talk straight.

I remember about my golden years as goal keeper at places where they no longer exist like in Bairro da Serafina where I have played with one older skilled goal keeper which could not enter our high school team because he was not a student.

Miss Maple is one German girl which has obsessive compulsive disorder and she tries hard to settle down her anxiety.

Patrícia Guerreiro is one case which lasts for more than 10 years and it will take time and patience to endure her path which is complex and original.

People in here like to cheat even when they talk, could not understand so far this word relation with logistics.

Time to think about sexuality and about being a father; does a father has quality time to fulfill its sexuality, I believe so, it is a matter of organization.

I remember Avózinha which had 97 years old when I have met her, she lived in Rua Conde das Antas and she had worked in New York on her youth. I do not want to point the guilt people who have forgotten her in the quarter of Campolide, namely in Estrela de Campolide from 2000 till 2004 more or less.

In Toulouse a murderer was shot, they could had arrested him and make me him a prisoner. It was strange because I know one French woman which is Jewish, maybe she has children; the day before I have emailed the Portuguese Unicef appealing to the defense of the children. In this morning some strange people passed on the street, I slept like a baby.

One good woman has protected me with her dog, one man passed and he was a gentleman. I was shy in the crowd. It is sunny, The Felt are on. What can I do with my libido when she is so strong? Milinha used to tell me that my mission is to help humans and animals, I just do not know at the moment how and I remember how I helped one old man from being spanked by German police.

Today I made Onanism for some time, walked enough, smiled at my will to move into a calm place, thought about the people which moved from this building, woke up sad because it seems that it needs some humorous mercy to understand the rising needs of this alphabet. Of course, the machos were passing after their incursion with women and the street was calm. The chaplain is somehow at the Hospital where he attends people, the birds sing aloud in here. Everything returns like Siddharta would say. One woman looked at me and the writer for 4 days does nothing than to read the newspaper, maybe he is a cop.

I dreamed while I was thinking and vice versa, it was difficult because my mind was confused for different reasons and had to take a cold shower in order to awake into my real and random way of coping with several dreams which tend to think and are no longer a mess.

I remember one colleague swallowing one fly, his name was Diogo Castro Santos and something, he became known in the mid 80´s due to the fact that he was a promise on F1 but he failed. My high school football team were champions for two years. Many of us were missing the classes to attend the matches and I used to organize a pile of old tiles to observe better the players. My team played with the best team from there and we were winning 1-0 as big surprise with one subtle goal by Leonel dos Santos Alves (perhaps the nephew of Mr. Carlos Celso dos Santos Alves), then we lost 1-14 because they were much stronger physically no matter how much we had tried to cope with the differences.

I have studied, waited for my dreams to suit reality, my sleeping time was good because I was tired due to the effort I have made for three hours around the studies of neurobiology, then the force of nature in the person of my mother came and I have refrained my studies into a deep sleep where many things took place and where I had my repose.

I feel alone in this city, I feel misunderstood especially when I am not teaching or healing, so I am at my kind of volition born from one scarlet music which is inside a singular ethic. Today I realized that many musicians spent time taking drugs and that what is left of them is an old cloth. The two physicians who live here are not now at the moment. Yesterday the girl moved. My hair reminds of my diary which was read by one tourist, she told me what sense made my words, I said nothing, and I had to wait. Later as I produced one of my best English poems, which took place at Bairro Alto where I wrote half of it (the other half was on the military bag of my favorite muse); it happened that I wanted to offer him into one tourist and she refused because she was looking for cheap sex rather than essence. I was lucky. At the time Carol Chomsky passed away, Professor Chomsky was touched by Wide Music, the poem.

From here I can see different shapes of the skies; it is one extraordinary motion especially when birds appear to observe human behavior. They are silent during the night, only garbage men and drunken people pass by from mid night through dawn until the morning breaks to salute the warmth from a beneficial prospect of the golden movement of peace.

The digestion of a pigeon when he looks into a similar dwelling upon humans, he figures out why we all stand for a logic based on biology which by normal conditions, it is conferred by the repose as a leaf does when Autumn arouses from many meadows being a variety of the nucleus like when I was going into the football matches, observing the trees and also knowing about the Walt Disney fans from Rua de Artilharia I.

When telemedicine will become global, then a better housing of the regular presence of goods will be the future design of who gathers hope as a clear credence.

I had one erection in my daily dreams and was making sodomy on one woman in my room in Escurquela.

The readings of Buddha led me to think that he was wrong because the sexual energy cannot be forgotten from the body.

I was thinking about studying medicine but my work with young and old people was done and I had found Orgon after 26 years of work. Now I need to settle my economy and to have Orgonomic thoughts while I think in many lives as my neighbor which is a physician. In those half dreams, I thought of the boys, who live in Kirchdorf/Jeeser, then my mother went and I really fell asleep with The Beatles. At the coffee place I looked at the TV and there were images of women, the customers were blocked, there were about 5 customers outside, one was familiar and the others no. On my awakening with caffeine I thought of Sharon which is too much connected with computers. She even wonders if computers dream, I guess that is one way for her to handle with things. Existence.

My parents saw the brains open of one man in Sátão. For years I thought that Paula Santos was Miss from this village. She was Miss Viseu in the late 80´s.

The couple which was painting the sunset near the Aqueduct in Lisbon and the woman in Greifswald, who was painting the local church, both have the beauty based on the sun, a good element of nature.

Latin word for disinhibition

Mon Jun 11, 2012 12:29 am

There is not in Latin the word for disinhibition.

The Medicine of Altruism

Sat Jun 09, 2012 6:37 am

In Tibet we say that many illness can be cured by the one medicine of love and compassion. These qualities are the ultimate source of human happiness, and need for them lies at the very core of our being. Unfortunately, love and compassion have been omitted from too many spheres of social interaction for too long. Usually confined to family and home, their practice in public life is considered impractical, even naive. This is tragic. In my view point, the practice of compassion is not just a symptom of unrealistic idealism but the most effective way to pursue the best interest of others as well as our own. The more we- as a nation, a group or as individuals - depend upon others, the more it is in our own best interests to ensure their well-being.

Practicing altruism is the real source of compromise and cooperation; merely recognizing our need for harmony is not enough. A mind committed to compassion is like an overflowing reservoir - a constant source of energy, determination and kindness. This is like a seed; when cultivated, gives rise to many other good qualities, such as forgiveness, tolerance, inner strength and the confidence to overcome fear and insecurity. The compassionate mind is like an elixir; it is capable of transforming bad situation into beneficial ones. Therefore, we should not limit our expressions of love and compassion to our family and friends. Nor is the compassion only the responsibility of clergy, health care and social workers. It is the necessary business of every part of the human community.

Whether a conflict lies in the field of politics, business or religion, an altruistic approach is frequently the sole means of resolving it. Sometimes the very concepts we use to meditate a dispute are themselves the cause of the problem. At such times, when a resolution seems impossible, both sides should recall the basic human nature that unites them. This will help break the impasse and, in the long run, make it easier for everyone to attain their goal. Although neither side may be fully satisfied, if both make concessions, at the very least, the danger of further conflict will be averted. We all know that this form of compromise is the most effective way of solving problems - why, then, do we not use it more often?

When I consider the lack of cooperation in human society, I can only conclude that it stems from ignorance of our interdependent nature. I am often moved by the example of small insects, such as bees. The laws of nature dictate that bees work together in order to survive. As a result, they possess an instinctive sense of social responsibility. They have no constitution, laws, police, religion or moral training, but because of their nature they labor faithfully together. Occasionally they may fight, but in general the whole colony survives based on cooperation. Human beings, on the other hand, have constitutions, vast legal systems and police forces; we have religion, remarkable intelligence and a heart with great capacity to love. But despite our many extraordinary qualities, in actual practice we lag behind those small insects; in some ways, I feel we are poorer than the bees.

For instance, millions of people live together in large cities all over the world, but despite this proximity, many are lonely. Some do not have even one human being with whom to share their deepest feelings, and live in a state of perpetual agitation. This is very sad. We are not solitary animals that associate only in order to mate. If we were, why would we build large cities and towns? But even though we are social animals compelled to live together, unfortunately, we lack sense of responsibility towards our fellow humans. Does the fault lie in our social architecture - the basic structures of family and community that support our society? Is it our own external facilities - our machines, science and technology? I do not think so.

I believe that despite the rapid advances made by civilization in this century, the most immediate cause of our present dilemma is our undue emphasis on material development alone. We have become so engrossed in its pursuit that, without even knowing it, we have neglected to foster the most basic human needs of love, kindness, cooperation and caring. If we do not know someone or find another reason for not feeling connected with a particular individual or group, we simply ignore them. But the development of human society is based entirely on people helping each other. Once we have lost the essential humanity that is our foundation, what is the point of pursuing only material improvement.

To me, it is clear: a genuine sense of responsibility can result only if we develop compassion. Only a spontaneous feeling of empathy for others can really motivate us to act on their behalf.

America's Overmedicated Children

Thu Jun 07, 2012 2:40 am

"Forgotten Children" is an investigative report by Carole Keeton Strayhorn,[1] the Texas Comptroller (2004) who uncovered evidence that 60% of children in the Texas foster care system are being drugged with powerful psychotropic drugs, most of which have not been tested in or approved for use by children. The Food and Drug Administration (FDA) acknowledges that many of these drugs have serious adverse side effects, both physical and psychological. The Comptroller said she was alarmed that in her review of a single month (November 2003), two powerful antipsychotic drugs -- Risperdal and Zyprexa -- made up half of the drugs prescribed to foster children in Texas. These two drugs have been approved only for adults for the treatment of psychosis - primarily schizophrenia - yet, she found that children as young as four, were receiving these powerful, mind-altering drugs.

The number of American children under 19 years of age who are prescribed psychotropic drugs is staggering - the use of these drugs eclipses all other categories for this age group. Between 2000 and 2003, the use of these drugs among teenagers increased threefold, and the number of children treated for "severe behavioral conditions" related to conduct disorder and autism jumped more than 60%.[2] The FDA estimates 11 million antidepressant prescriptions were written in 2003 for under 19 year old's--a 27% increase in 3 years. Drugs used primarily to treat attention deficit/ hyperactivity (ADHD), which remains a controversial "condition," increased the most. In 5 to 9 year old children the use of drugs increased 85%, and in preschoolers usage was up 49%.[3] Physicians prescribe mind-altering drugs even as they know that for this age group the developing brain is undergoing extraordinary changes. They acknowledge: "we have very little information about the long-term impact of treatment with these drugs early in development."[4]

The unprecedented number of children being diagnosed with psychiatric conditions, then prescribed psychotropic drugs can be traced to the collaborative efforts of the drug industry and its paid collaborators: professional associations of psychiatrists, leading psychiatrists at prestigious universities, and government health care agencies that are financially dependent on drug companies. Beginning in the 1990s a series of federally sponsored "mental health" initiatives promoted the idea that children's mental health was in crisis, [5] that they were suffering from undiagnosed depression, and that early treatment is essential to prevent suicide. These influential collaborators flooded the channels of communication with misinformation, persuading doctors and parents that children's mental health was a major problem and that "safe and effective" remedies were at hand.

Hundreds of news stories including dozens of peer reviewed journal articles repeated the message: the new antidepressants, Prozac and its cousins--sertraline (Zoloft), seroxat (Paxil) - were described as "safe and effective" "magic bullets." Unlike the old imprecise, sedating antidepressants, these drugs, we were told, are "selective serotonin reuptake inhibitors" (SSRIs) - the implication being that they act with precision on the serotonin receptors. Parents were misled to believe that SSRIs were "safe and effective and well tolerated in children,"[6] when they had shown no benefit greater than placebo, while producing severe adverse effects in children. A mental health epidemic was created (critics believe) to provide an expanded market for new drugs. Even infants and toddlers are prescribed Prozac with the blessing of the medical / psychiatric establishment. In 1998, an FDA contracted survey found that 3,000 Prozac prescriptions had been written for infants. [7]

Of note: Before Prozac antidepressants had been used only for severely depressed, hospitalized patients who were at high risk of suicide. The advent of Prozac changed all that - anyone expressing a sign of unhappiness, anxiety, or moodiness from the ebb and flow of life, was diagnosed as suffering from depression. When tested in controlled trials, the new generation antidepressants have failed to demonstrate a benefit either for severely depressed hospitalized patients or for troubled children. The business success of Prozac is attributable to creative aggressive marketing. However, the new antidepressants - SSRIs and SNRIs (selective serotonin norepinephrine reuptake inhibitors) --pose significant life-threatening risks of harm which, for almost two decades, had been concealed from the public. The most serious documented harm links SSRIs /SNRIs to increased risk of suicide and violence in youth.

Prescribing physicians in Europe and the US were kept in the dark about the serious risks until paroxetine (Paxil) was exposed by the BBC (2003). The drug was shown to cause severe withdrawal symptoms - a sign of drug dependency - and it triggered violent outbursts and suicide. The UK medicines authority (MHRA)[8] was first to issue a public warning about the dangers of Paxil in June 2003, and to ban the use of SSRIs / SNRIs in children, save Prozac. In March 2004, the US FDA[9] followed, issuing extensive bold warnings about the increased risk of suicidal behavior in both children and adults who take an antidepressant - for any condition "psychiatric or non-psychiatric." In October 2004,[10] the FDA issued black box warnings about the twofold increased risks of suicidal behavior in youth taking any antidepressant, including Prozac.

The European Medicines Agency (EMA) [11] is the last regulatory agency to catch up. In April (2005), the EMA's scientific committee (CMHU) issued a press release recommending warnings on the labels of all the new SSRI / SNRI antidepressants to reflect the evidence: "SSRIs/SNRIs should not be used in the treatment of children and adolescents unless specifically authorized. Suicide-related behaviors (suicide attempt and suicidal thoughts), and hostility (predominantly aggression, oppositional behavior and anger) were more frequently observed in clinical trials among children and adolescents treated with antidepressants compared to those treated with placebo." The EMA added Strattera (atomoxetine) to the list of drugs prescribed for children, noting its "lack of efficacy in depression." Strattera is approved only for the treatment of ADHD for adults and children: but it poses increased risks which constitute the very symptoms that constitute a diagnosis of ADHD: "hostility, aggression, oppositional behavior, and anger."

Antipsychotics are the most powerful, most toxic psychotropic drugs that have neither been tested in, nor approved for use by children, yet they are the second most widely prescribed drugs for children. Although the scientific evidence for their effectiveness is tenuous, nevertheless, these powerful drugs are widely prescribed primarily for off-label uses. Antipsychotics were approved for the treatment of psychosis in adults, primarily for schizophrenia and short-term use for bipolar disorder. These drugs induce severe, potentially fatal adverse effects and now carry FDA required warnings that they impair judgment, thinking, and motor skills. Since 2003 the labels carry black box warnings about potentially fatal diabetes mellitus, especially in youth. They also carry risks of prolonged heart QT interval, cardiac arrhythmia and stroke. Antipsychotics are the fourth highest selling class of prescribed drugs in the US-- sales in 2002 reached $6.4 billion.2 The greatest spending increase for the treatment of children diagnosed with behavior problems, is due to skyrocketing use of the most expensive drugs to treat ADHD, conduct disorder, autism, and affective disorders such as depression.

These drugs are known to induce severe, potentially fatal adverse effects and now carry FDA required warnings about the risks of cardiac arrhythmias, impaired judgment, thinking, and motor skills. Since 2003 the labels carry black box warnings about potentially fatal diabetes mellitus, especially in youth. Concerns are being raised about why young people who are not psychotic are being prescribed these powerful drugs for unapproved uses without evidence of their safety.

Investigations across the US corroborate the abusive use of psychotropic drugs:

The Massachusetts Behavioral Health Partnership[12] reported that almost two thirds of children in state care were treated for behavioral disorders in 2003.

An analysis of the medical records of 300,000 children aged 2 through 18 who were enrolled in the Tennessee Medicaid healthcare program for the poor and uninsured found that the use of antipsychotics for children nearly doubled in six years. Nearly one in every 100 adolescents covered under the Tennessee program was being prescribed antipsychotics in 2001. The increases were most dramatic among children aged 6 to 12 (a 93% rise) and those aged 13 to 18 (a 116% increase). The use of antipsychotics among preschool children increased 61%[13].

An investigative series in Columbus Ohio[14] found that 40,000 children aged 6-18 who were covered by Medicaid were prescribed psychotropic drugs: 31% of those children were in foster care, and 22% were in juvenile detention. Medicaid spent $65.5 million for drugs used primarily as "chemical restraints." Among these: Chelsey Kennedy, 15, says she "slept for four days and was in a drug-induced fog for a week" after being subdued with three shots of a powerful drug at a Dayton treatment center. Now she's at a Columbus center, but her mother worries about the number of medications she takes daily - 14, of which 11 are psychotropic drugs, compared with two when she went into treatment two years ago.

A 10-year-old boy was chemically restrained 69 times over 80 days. Doctors prescribed up to six drugs at a time - no one has ever determined which pills worked for what symptoms or disorders.

A 12-year-old girl was injected six times over nine months with high doses of Thorazine, a powerful sedative that can knock kids out and cause painful muscle spasms and twitches. She also was physically restrained 31 times by as many as three men, despite a history of being physically and sexually abused.

A Texas mother reported that starting at age five her son was variously diagnosed as suffering from ADHD, bipolar disorder, schizophrenia, or sociopathy - diagnosis depended on the doctor in charge. The boy was put on powerful psychotropic drugs which, she says, made him hear voices, and resulted in troubles in school, with the law, and repeated hospitalizations. When he was put on Zyprexa "he put on a tremendous amount of weight, 85 pounds to be exact."[15] Since being weaned off the drugs, she reported that her son is much improved.

A five month investigation by the Tampa Florida Tribune[16] shows how prescribing psychiatric drugs mistakenly can precipitate life-threatening tragedies. For example, 9- year old Lee who had been diagnosed with bipolar disorder descended into suicidal violence after she had been haphazardly prescribed a combination of four powerful drugs - two antidepressants and two antipsychotics. She developed an obsessive fear of germs, for which the psychiatrist suggested an antidepressant (Paxil). Within weeks, Lee's mother noticed a surge in her aggression. She told the doctor, but he said it was an acceptable side effect and she would be fine. Well, she was not fine: "Emergency workers cornered her behind the office and tied her to a gurney. She screamed and thrashed the whole way to the Community Hospital emergency room and screamed throughout the afternoon as nurses tried to sedate her. They finally succeeded by giving her a shot of Thorazine."

How can such abuse possibly be therapeutic for any 9-year-old child? /li>

A series in the California Sacramento Bee[17] described what happened to 12-year old Zach during a period of 18 months. Zach was diagnosed with anxiety, depression and ADHD: he was first prescribed Ritalin, then Prozac, then paroxetine (Paxil) which made him manic. Then, he was back to Prozac plus the antipsychotic, Zyprexa, which made him gain 40 lbs. within 5 months. He was then prescribed quitiapine (Seroquel), the dose was raised but his psychiatrist said he is "disappointed" because Zach is still irritable, so he's considering the newest antipsychotic, ziprasidone (Geodon). The drug label carries bold warnings about rapid heartbeats and cardiac arrest: "sudden unexplained deaths have been reported in patients taking ziprasidone at recommended doses."

A Dallas Fort Worth investigation[18] found that in one month (November 2003), some doctors were writing as many as 486 prescriptions for psychotropic drugs for children in foster care. One psychiatrist explained to the reporter in an e-mail: "I am often pressured by providers to aggressively medicate children in an attempt to control their behavior."

Dr. Ellen Bassuk, professor at Harvard University who examined children's medical records said: "It's scandalous that medications are used to subdue kids for the convenience of overworked and underpaid staff or as punishment for bad behavior."[14] The Texas comptroller agrees: she believes the drugs are prescribed for children in order to make them "more docile." And, she deplores that "doctors and drug companies are pushing them to make a buck." And a neuropsychologist from Florida who examined the Texas records[19] said that by numbing children with psychotropic drugs:

"We're taking away their future." By blunting their emotion, we take away children's ability to relate to people, to trust, love, to care for others or to put themselves in another person's shoes to see how it feels.

To make matters even worse, the US government has begun to implement a mental health screening policy recommended by the President's New Freedom Commission on Mental Health[20] (NFC). According to the BMJ,[21] President Bush instructed more than 25 federal agencies to develop an implementation plan to screen America's 52 million school children and 6 million school personnel - for hidden mental illness. The rationale behind this mind-boggling initiative is, in part, evidence of America's abiding faith in science and technology to provide solutions for complex human and societal problems. In no other democratic country has the government adopted a policy to screen the entire population - children first - for presumed, undetected, mental illness.

The methodology used to screen for mental and behavioral problems remains rooted in the flawed methods used by the discredited eugenics movement which sought to screen for mental "defectives." Eugenics and psychiatry suffer from a common philosophical fallacy that undermines the validity of their theories and their prescriptions. Both are rooted in "faith-based" ideological assumptions that mental and behavior problems are biologically determined, and can, therefore, be resolved through biological interventions.

However, the diagnosis of mental illness lacks scientific validity - it relies entirely on the subjective assessment by mental health professionals and normative check lists. This flaw was acknowledged by the US Surgeon General report:[22] "mental health is not easy to defineï¿½.what it means to be mentally healthy is subject to many different interpretations that are rooted in value judgments that may vary across cultures." Another shortcoming: mental health professionals have an interest in expanding the patient roster to guarantee their employment. Therefore, screening will most likely inflate the number of American children (and adults) labeled with a mental illness.

The New Freedom Commission Report praised two mental health programs: TeenScreen and TMAP. TeenScreen is a questionnaire devised by psychiatrists at Columbia University "to ensure that every teen in the US has access to free mental health check-up." TeenScreen is already operating in more than 100 schools in 34 states and as the executive director told a congressional committee: "In 2003, we were able to screen approximately 14,200 teens...; among those students, we were able to identify approximately 3,500 youth with mental health problems and link them with treatment. This year, we believe we will be able to identify close to 10,000 teens in need, a 300 percent increase over last year." Unfortunately, this is not science fiction: this is a policy driven by commercial interests.

TMAP (Texas Medication Algorithm Project) is an industry sponsored set of flow charts designed to guide mental health providers' selection of psychotropic drugs-- "Psychiatry for Dummies." TMAP was launched in 1995, when Bush was governor of Texas. TMAP recommends the most expensive drugs as first line treatment - these are the SSRI and SSNRI antidepressants and antipsychotics. At least twelve states have adopted the TMAP model: Texas and Ohio were among the first. State mental health officials across the US see nothing wrong with prescribing drugs irresponsibly, thereby violating medicine's first principle--"do no harm" - to increase profits. Of note, Ohio's executive director of the Department of Mental Health, Michael Hogan, who has played a major role in promoting the use of psychotropic drugs, was chairman of the New Freedom Commission. He said that although: "It's true children are more likely to get medication than counseling or other behavioral therapy, at the end of the day, meds re quite safe and effective."14 Hogan says the biggest danger facing children is depression.

Screening for mental illness serves no medical purpose - it is but the first step toward expanded use of drugs. Given its large margin of error, screening for mental illness is of dubious value for individuals, but that same margin of error is of great value for the drug industry. An evaluation by the authoritative US Preventive Services Task Force[23] concluded that the mental health screening instruments have not been validated, and there is no evidence to demonstrate that screening reduces suicide. The escalating expenditure for psychotropic drugs since TMAP leaves little doubt as to its value for the drug industry. The impact of TMAP[24] is already evident in the skyrocketing increased prescriptions for antipsychotics which are being prescribed widely for unapproved, off-label uses, mostly to control conduct and behavior, including ADHD. US spending for drugs to treat ADHD rose astronomically3: among 5 to 9-year old's spending rose 174%, and for preschool children spending rose by 369%. These extraordinary spending increases reflect the increased use of the most expensive drugs to treat newly minted behavioral problems in children who are increasingly diagnosed with ADHD and bipolar disorder (a.k.a. manic-depression).

Indeed, the Wall Street Journal[25] reported last week: "The number of children diagnosed as bipolar rose 26% from 2002 to 2004, to 19,776 cases," noting that until recently, children under 18 were very rarely diagnosed with bipolar disorder. Yet, today, children as young as four are being diagnosed with bipolar. The Journal also notes that: "increased use of antipsychotic medicines, such as Seroquel and Risperdal, was a big driver of pediatric drug costs last year." Indeed, overall spending on psychotropic drugs for children increased by 77%, and increased by 142% for "severe conduct disorder."

Screening will do much to expand the number of patients relegated to mental health providers and to increase profit margins for drug manufacturers. In the last two years, 107,000 children in Texas have been prescribed psychotropic drugs at a cost of $167 million. The experience of 15-year old Aliah Gleason, encapsulates the abuse a child is likely to be subjected to after being screened and (often as not) misdiagnosed as having a mental disorder. Her story is reported in Mother Jones. [26]

MEDICATING ALIAH (excerpt)

In the early part of seventh grade, Aliah was a B and C student who got in trouble "for running my mouth." School officials considered Aliah disruptive, deemed her to have an "oppositional disorder," and placed her in a special education track. Her parents viewed her as a spirited child who was bright but with a tendency to argue and clown. Then one day, psychologists from the University of Texas (UT) visited the school to conduct a mental health screening for sixth- and seventh-grade girls, and Aliah's life took a dramatic turn.

A few weeks later, the Gleasons got a "Dear parents" form letter from the head of the screening program. "You will be glad to know your daughter did not report experiencing a significant level of distress," it said. Not long after, they got a very different phone call from a UT psychologist, who told them Aliah had scored high on a suicide rating and needed further evaluation. The Gleasons reluctantly agreed to have Aliah see a UT consulting psychiatrist. She concluded that Aliah was suicidal but did not hospitalize her, referring her instead to an emergency clinic for further evaluation. Six weeks later, in January 2004, a child-protection worker went to Aliah's school, interviewed her, then summoned her father to the school and told him to take Aliah to Austin State Hospital, a state mental facility. He refused, and after a heated conversation, Aliah was placed in emergency custody and a police officer drove her to the hospital.

The Gleasons would not be allowed to see or even speak to their daughter for the next five months. Aliah would spend a total of nine months in a state psychiatric hospital and residential treatment facilities. While in the hospital, she was placed in restraints more than 26 times and medicated-against her will and without her parents' consent-with at least 12 different psychiatric drugs, many of them simultaneously.

On her second day at the state hospital, Aliah says she was told to take a pill to "help my mood swings." She refused and hid under her bed. She says staff members pulled her out by her legs, then told her if she took her medication, she'd be able to go home sooner. She took it. On another occasion, she "cheeked" a pill and later tossed it into the garbage. She says that after staff members found it, five of them came to her room, one holding a needle. "I started struggling, and they held my head down and shot me in the butt," she says. "Then they left and I lay in my bed crying."

What, if anything, was wrong with Aliah remains cloudy. Court documents and medical records indicate that she would say she was suicidal or that her father beat her, and then she would recant. (Her attorney attributes such statements to the high dosages of psychotropic drugs she was forcibly put on.) Her clinical diagnosis was just as changeable. During two months at Austin State Hospital, Aliah was diagnosed with "depressive disorder not otherwise specified," "mood disorder not otherwise specified with psychotic features," and "major depression with psychotic features."

In addition to the antidepressants Zoloft, Celexa, Lexapro, and Desyrel, as well as Ativan, an antianxiety drug, Aliah was given two newer drugs known as "atypical antipsychotics"--Geodon and Abilify--plus an older antipsychotic, Haldol. She was also given the anticonvulsants Trileptal and Depakote-though she was not suffering from a seizure disorder-and Cogentin, an anti-Parkinson's drug also used to control the side effects of antipsychotic drugs. At the time of her transfer to a residential facility, she was on five different medications, and once there, she was put on still another atypical-Risperdal.

At times Aliah "was on five different medications, putting her on the extreme end of a growing practice known as polypharmacy that worries many doctors." Dr. Joseph Woolston, a Yale University professor and chief of child psychiatry at Yale said: "If you or I were on that regimen we would have a lot of trouble attending to work or school. We don't have any idea what that combination of medications does to a developing child. It may have a number of long-term side effects." He also suspects "that the drugs may have been used as much to control the angry reactions of a girl who was hospitalized against her will as to treat any mental and emotional problems."

Aliah was a victim of mental health screening. Screening for mental illness serves no medical or societal purpose - screening will, however, do much to increase the profit margins for drug manufacturers and the mental health provider industry. A label of mental illness all too often signifies loss of autonomous decision-making authority for parents who may be reluctant to give permission for their children to be treated with psychotropic drugs.

A dark side of screening is the stigma that accompanies those labeled as having a mental disorder. Being so classified all too often signifies loss of autonomy and decision-making authority. Parents who are reluctant to give permission for their children to be treated with psychotropic drugs - such as Aliah Gleason's parents - face state agents who impose their authority over parental objections. American psychiatry is treading down the same slippery slope that the eugenics movement did in its heyday. Psychiatry, like eugenics, is armed with an arsenal of unproven bio-genetic theories and assumptions about human behavior. Eugenicists blamed heredity for bad behavior: psychiatrists blame unproven faulty brain chemistry. Eugenics imposed radical interventions against the will of the individuals targeted - so does psychiatry.

Eugenicists and psychiatrists have done incalculable harm because their "treatments" were sanctioned by a government seal providing the illusion of legitimacy. In the US, state Eugenics boards approved the involuntary sterilization of 72,600 people who had been classified (often arbitrarily) as "mental defectives."[27] Psychiatry uses state agents to coerce parents to force children to ingest drugs that disrupt normal brain function.

Questions:

Who will bear responsibility for the harms that may follow from mental health screening when children are wrongly labeled as having a mental illness, and on that basis, will be prescribed mind-altering drugs that cause them harm?

Who will compensate children who will be deprived of a normal childhood?

Vera Sharav

Which American has the courage?

Tue Jun 05, 2012 3:14 pm

Alexander emailed the Wilhelm Reich Infant Trust in order to donate 100 000 USD from the selling of land in Escurquela if justice were made into the humanist according to their courage to pressure the American government, no answer came.

Vicissitudes of Psychiatry's Diagnostic Manual Revisions

Tue Jun 05, 2012 2:48 pm

Monday, 14 May 2012

The latest area of controversy focuses on the proposed revision of the definition "behavioral addiction disorder" extending the addiction diagnosis to include drug, alcohol and gambling. It is estimated that the change would expand the number of people labeled as "addicts" by 20 to 30 million who would be entitled to treatment and disability payments costing taxpayers many hundreds of millions of dollars.

The proposed revisions to the Diagnostic Statistical Manual (DSM) of the American Psychiatric Association will continue the trend set by prior revisions: namely, expanding the number of people who, according to DSM diagnostic criteria, will be labeled as having a "mental disorder" for which a prescription for psychotropic drugs will be issued. Indeed, the chairman of the DSM-IV Task Force recently wrote: "The relentless march to medicalize normality out of existence is opening a new and especially ridiculous front."

The latest area of controversy focuses on the proposed revision of the definition "behavioral addiction disorder" extending the addiction diagnosis to include drug, alcohol and gambling. It is estimated that the change would expand the number of people labeled as "addicts" by 20 to 30 million who would be entitled to treatment and disability payments costing taxpayers many hundreds of millions of dollars. APA's chief executive, Dr. James Scully, Jr., defends the expansionist revision by reiterating the hackneyed claim that "The biggest problem in all of psychiatry is untreated illness, and that has huge social costs." New Guidelines May Sharply Increase Addiction Diagnoses

Insightful critics have observed that the designation "mental disorder" for inclusion in each of the revised editions of the DSM can be traced to the availability of a drug that will be marketed as a remedy for the newly invented "mental disorder." Indeed, the DSM is a driving force for rendering every human emotion and behavior that can be affected in one way or another by a psychotropic drug, to be classified as a symptom of a mental disorder. More than anything else, the DSM catapulted clinically ineffective drugs--such as, SSRI antidepressants and (atypical) neuroleptics into industry's most profitable blockbuster drugs—even as they have caused severe harm.

The DSM has been described as "a hideous distortion of medical science"--its objective is expansive and self-serving. The New York Times report by Ian Urbina (May 12, 2012) perfectly captures the seeming lack of insight (dishonesty?) displayed by psychiatrists when questioned about their financial conflicts of interest. Urbina reports:

"Dr. Charles O'Brien [University of Pennsylvania] who led the addiction working group, has been a consultant for several pharmaceutical companies, including Pfizer, GlaxoSmithKline and Sanofi-Aventis, all of which make drugs marketed to combat addiction. He has also worked extensively as a paid consultant for Alkermes, a pharmaceutical company, studying a drug, Vivitrol, that combats alcohol and heroin addiction by preventing craving. He was the driving force behind adding "craving" to the new manual's list of recognized symptoms of addiction."

"I'm quite proud to have played a role, because I know that craving plays such an important role in addiction," Dr. O'Brien said, adding that he had never made any money from the sale of drugs that treat craving. New Guidelines May Sharply Increase Addiction Diagnoses Surely such an indication of dissociation must qualify for a DSM diagnosis and a psychotropic drug.

The DSM-I, published in 1952, included 106 disorders; the DSM-II, published in 1968, included 182 disorders; the DSM-III, published in 1980, included 265 disorders: its architect, Dr. Robert Spitzer of Columbia University, dropped psychoanalytic theories and concepts such as "reaction" and "neurosis" and replaced them with a classification system of descriptive diagnostic categories. Since the DSM III, diagnoses of mental disorders are determined by symptom classifications using a system of checklists. A major flaw is the assumption that discreet mental disorders can be deduced from symptom patterns without regard for context or life stressors that may impact a human being's state of mind.

The DSM-III simplification of the diagnostic criteria resulted in millions of normal people to be mislabeled as having a "mental disorder." The global influence of DSM-III surpassed all previous editions. The DSM became the primary determinant of treatment decisions, private and public insurance and disability eligibility, government funding for special education services, it is relied upon as a guide for pharmaceutical research, and has been widely used by criminal defense lawyers.

In a BBC interview, 27 years after the publication of the DSM-III, Dr.

Spitzer acknowledged that the DSM diagnostic criteria resulted in "exaggerated rates of mental disorders." When asked what the rate of exaggeration might be? He acknowledged that "no one really knows, but it might be 20%, 30%, even 40%."

http://www.spring.org.uk/2007/03/why-it ... etimes.php

Two opinion pieces about the DSM-5 revisions were published by the two most influential American newspapers. The Washington Post published an essay by Paula Caplan, PhD, "Psychiatry's Bible, the DSM, is Doing More Harm Than Good" (April 27, 2012) and The New York Times, ran an OpEd by Allen Frances, MD, "Diagnosing the DSM" (May 12, 2012).

Dr. Allen Frances, former chairman of psychiatry at Duke University who chaired the DSM-IV revision published in 1994, contributed toward further increasing the number of people diagnosed with a mental disorder--the number of disorders had grown to 297. Worst of all, the DSM-IV ushered in an epidemic of child abuse under the guise of medical intervention. After the loosened DSM-IV diagnostic criteria pathologized normal childhood behavior, millions of children have been labeled with attention deficit disorder, autism spectrum disorder, and bipolar disorder, for which psychiatrists have been wantonly prescribing toxic drugs whose documented, severe adverse effects induced debilitating chronic physical disease, not to mention mental deterioration, and premature deaths.

After the damage had been done--and billions of dollars had been misspent on harm-producing treatments--Dr. Frances acknowledges in the Times OpEd that the DSM-IV had "failed to anticipate or control the faddish over-diagnosis of autism, attention deficit disorders and bipolar disorder in children." Elsewhere, he has expressed horror about the resulting consequences: "kids getting unneeded antipsychotics that would make them gain 12 pounds in 12 weeks hit me in the gut. It was uniquely my job and my duty to protect them. If not me to correct it, who? I was stuck without an excuse." He has also criticized psychiatry's ever expanding list of invalidated disease designations, its reliance on demonstrably ham-producing drugs, and has acknowledged in an interview in WIRED that, "there is no definition of a mental disorder. . . . These concepts are virtually impossible to define precisely."

Dr. Caplan, a clinical psychologist who served on two committees of the DSM-IV (until she resigned in protest about the pathologizing of per-menstrual cramps) has been a vocal critic about its lack of a scientific foundation:

"An undeserved aura of scientific precision surrounds the manual: It has "statistical" in its title and includes a precise-seeming three- to five-digit code for every diagnostic category and subcategory, as well as lists of symptoms a patient must have to receive a diagnosis. But what it does is simply connect certain dots, or symptoms — such as sadness, fear or insomnia — to construct diagnostic categories that lack scientific grounding. Many therapists see patients through the DSM prism, trying to shoehorn a human being into a category."

She has also criticized the DSM's overreaching stranglehold: Psychiatry estimates that within their lifetime, 50% of the American population will be "diagnosed" with a mental disorder. A psychiatric label, Dr. Caplan points out, causes serious harm:

"it can cost anyone their health insurance, job, custody of their children, or right to make their own medical and legal decisions. And if patients take psychiatric drugs, they risk developing physical disorders such as diabetes, heart problems, weight gain and other serious conditions."

Dr. Frances has become the most formidable vocal critic of the DSM-5 Task Force and its proposed revisions who was influential in persuading the Task Force to pull-back from adopting the diagnosis "psychosis risk syndrome" that would have expanded even further the prescribing of dangerous toxic drugs for children, and the proposal to eliminate the bereavement exclusion from major depressive episode (MDE) diagnosis which would have included just about everyone who ever mourned the loss of a loved one.

Those who formulated the DSM-III, -IV and 5 are stakeholders with significant financial interests in increasing the number of patients and in the drugs used to treat the diagnoses that they alone define in the DSM. What's more, the APA leadership influences public health policy.

But Dr. Frances has a blind spot in regard to the commercial interests that drive the entire enterprise. He steadfastly denies that financial interests had any influence on the crafting of the DSM even as he acknowledges that "the DSM drives the direction of research and the approval of new drugs." He denies industry's influence on the DSM-IV or DSM-5 Task Force, claiming that "mistakes are the result of intellectual conflicts of interest" not financial conflicts of interests."

Surely Dr. Frances is not unaware of the peer reviewed analysis by Dr. Lisa Cosgrove (Harvard University) and Dr. Sheldon Krimsky (Tufts University) documenting the financial ties of each committee of the DSM-IV (2006), and their comparison analysis of DSM-IV and DSM-5 panel members' financial ties to industry. Their DSM-IV findings:

"Our inquiry into the relationships between DSM-IV panel members and the pharmaceutical industry demonstrates that there are strong financial ties between the industry and those who are responsible for developing and modifying the diagnostic criteria for mental illness. Of the 170 DSM panel members 95 (56%) had financial ties to pharmaceutical companies. The connections are especially strong in those diagnostic areas where drugs are the first line of treatment for mental disorders. One hundred percent of the members of the panels on 'Mood Disorders' and 'Schizophrenia and Other Psychotic Disorders' had financial ties to drug companies. The leading categories of financial interest held by panel members were research funding (42%), consultancies (22%) and speaker's bureau (16%).

Drs. Cosgrove and Krimsky's comparison study of the DSM-IV and DSM-5 panel financial interests found, ironically, that APA's financial disclosure policy adopted for the DSM-5 panel was not accompanied by a reduction of financial conflicts. Instead, the financial ties to industry INCREASED from 56% to 70%. Furthermore, APA's disclosure requirement excludes speakers' bureau membership which provide fees for key opinion leaders (KOLs) who make presentations promoting products. Also exempt from APA's disclosure requirement are "unrestricted research grants."

As Rob Waters wrote in Salon Magazine: "The fight over the DSM-5 pits some of the biggest egos in the world of psychiatry, but it's more than a battle among 301.81s (narcissistic personality disorder). For people seeking help for life's problems who don't want to be labeled mentally ill or have their treatment limited to medication, and for clinicians who want to help people without reducing them to a category, the stakes are high."

Vera Sharav

References:
1. Cosgrove, L., Krimsky, S., Vijayraghavan, M. & Schneider, L. (2006). Financial ties between DSM-IV panel members and the pharmaceutical industry . Psychotherapy and Psychosomatics, 75, 154-160.
2. Cosgrove, L., Krimsky, S. (2012) A Comparison of DSM-IV and DSM-5 Panel Members' Financial Associations with Industry : A Pernicious Problem Persists, PLoS Medicine.

Karate: the ideal time for children's beginning

Sat Jun 02, 2012 12:29 pm

The recommended minimum age to start karate practice is 5 years. At this age the child has the ability to develop the notion of laterality (left, right, front, rear), speed (fast, slow) and the lap times of the movements / techniques (one, two, three, etc.) coordinated with the breath.

The Karate component that contains psycho-motor skills, promotes the development of the child regarding their self-confidence, sociability, decreased self-centeredness, and channel their energy. The health maintenance and strengthening of physical stimulation to the courage not to avoid the obstacles themselves, respect for others, balance and postures are characteristics that karate provides and that can be taught from this age. Because children tend to absorb everything around them, this is the best time to start learning the rules, customs, techniques, behaviors, etc.., Taught when practicing Karate.

The treasures of justice narrate the delicacy with fiction

Wed May 30, 2012 2:53 pm

In my youth, I used to make telepathy with one girl who lived in front of my room where a garden stands beautifully with cats, orange trees, birds and I could see the clouds and the stars.

In here I can see the stars and the moon alike the August in Escurquela with my character being understood as one measure of a quality judgment of a calm combination with a conspicuous passing present where all ethics must prevail in a noble manner as spiritual gratification to be studied. There is no need to ease the calm from the excitement of ardor in the same organization of the hopes and prospects being accepted as a sweet heart taken hold of the fury of this age, especially when the force does not heal but it triggers sadness. Eggshell powder is a good remedy into the body, it prevents as well as honey, the healthy laces of a personal history of each individual. As for animals, they need to live in calm wherever they are enjoying nature. One single mistake can record a social event printing the mission on what is and for a genius, the view to understand the infinite. After infinite, we all know. Rigor mortis is one element of logic which particles of having the solution for eternity. I have found this on my studies. Children do not like coffee, they have one golden imagination, and they express the innocent poetry giving expedition into their enterprises. The treasures of justice narrate the delicacy with fiction and fiction used to amuse and to have readers, those days on which the Out Space was thought are away as reputation of world problems.

Yoga for Children

Fri May 25, 2012 9:33 am

Quote from a Yoga School: after consulting our Yoga teachers they are unanimous in saying that only after the age of 14 years is that a child should practice yoga due to the action that yoga has on the endocrine system.

Striving to define normal

Mon May 21, 2012 3:41 pm

By Karen Weintraub
Dr. Jordan Smoller

Smoller, an associate professor of psychiatry at Harvard Medical School and Massachusetts General Hospital, has just written a book called "The Other Side of Normal."
Q. You write in your book that psychiatrists are just starting to try to understand what it means to have "normal" mental health. Why is it important to understand normalcy?
'Normal and abnormal are like night and day. We recognize that they're two different states, but the exact line between them is sort of impossible to draw.'
A. The biology of normal teaches us about both our everyday life and also mental illness. Many psychiatric disorders are variations of some of the

104

same brain systems that we use to navigate the challenges of everyday life. There's really a vast spectrum of normal in terms of how we adapt to life. By understanding that, by having a basic map of how the brain and the mind work, we can start to make sense of things, demystify and hopefully treat disorders that cause people a lot of suffering.

Q. How can we distinguish between normalcy and illness?

A. Normal and abnormal are like night and day. We recognize that they're two different states, but the exact line between them is sort of impossible to draw. We're comfortable with the fuzziness of twilight and that's probably where we're going to end up [with mental illness]. That doesn't mean psychiatric disorders are inventions or myths. We know that there are extremes of some of these traits or behaviors that cause people real pain and suffering.

Q. Are there examples of where having a definition of "normal" will make a difference in understanding disease?

A. We have circuits in our brain for detecting danger and harm. That's entirely normal. Sometimes [these systems] are active in the face of situations that are not really dangerous and they can take on a life of their own, they can go awry or go into overdrive. That is essentially what's happening in many anxiety disorders.

Q. So understanding "normal" anxiety can help us understand where anxiety becomes pathological?

A. It was an understanding of how the brain lays down emotional memories that led to a new avenue for treatment. [D-Cycloserine], a drug originally developed to treat tuberculosis enhances the function of emotional memory circuits. There have now been several studies suggesting that taking this pill an hour before cognitive behavioral therapy can boost effectiveness of therapies for panic disorder, obsessive compulsive disorder, and post-traumatic stress disorder.

Q. What role does life experience play in mental health?

A. At a neural level and even at a molecular level, experience — especially early experience — seems to affect the programming of our stress hormone systems, and how our genes tend to turn on and off.

Q. If early childhood is so crucial to future mental health, doesn't that put even more pressure on parents to get it right?

A. The brain is lying in wait for information that will help it organize basic functions like language and vision and emotional and social kinds of systems. But it's waiting for the ingredients that have been present throughout evolution — the presence of a caregiver, some degree of nurturing, some degree of exposure to language, exposure to social information. In the presence of that, kids do well. It's not about perfection.

Q. But adversity in childhood can have terrible effects on later life?

A. Real adversity and toxic stress, maltreatment and deprivation — those kinds of things especially early in life can have long-lasting effects. We know there is plasticity throughout life — the brain responds to the environment. That gives us a lot of hope that even if there has been adversity or difficulty early in life, there are things we can to help restore the course towards health."

The Alliance for Human Research Protection

Wed May 16, 2012 8:48 pm

Mission Statement

The Alliance for Human Research Protection (AHRP) is a national network of lay people and professionals dedicated to advancing responsible and ethical medical research practices, to minimizing the risks associated with such endeavors and to ensuring that the human rights, dignity and welfare of human subjects are protected

Board of Directors

This year, more than 15 million Americans will be recruited into clinical trials.

The AHRP mission is to stand up - and speak out - for the human rights of research subjects - especially those who are vulnerable and /or susceptible to coercion, manipulation and exploitation. Those who are incapable of exercising their right to informed consent are in greatest need of protection from research abuse

Disadvantaged children are sought as human guinea pigs - even toddlers and infants, some living in foster care;

Elderly people with impaired reasoning capacity, some living in nursing homes;

People disabled by mental or physical illness;

Illegal immigrants and disadvantaged populations living in

underdeveloped countries;

Prisoners, including members of the armed forces.

AHRP is the best-known, most visible, proactive citizens' watchdog organization bringing to public attention - through our daily Infomails - issues affecting the safety of people in clinical trials.

The AHRP's Unique Contribution:

We provide a public awareness forum through education, media exposure, and appeals to conscience and social justice, by,

Spearheading an educational campaign for informed consent to empower ordinary citizens with information they can use to better protect themselves and their children from undue risks of harm. Join our Campaign for Informed Consent.

Providing prospective research subjects with information and a questionnaire designed to inform them of their rights and responsibilities, thereby enhancing the process of informed consent. [link]

Sending alerts to professional groups, the media, and political leaders about violations of ethical standards in medical research.

Presenting the general public with timely, relevant information in a sustained educational effort.

Calling for reforms to improve clinical research designs and oversight.

Developing a web-based library and clearinghouse of resource materials for the use of both clinical investigators performing research on human subjects and the potential subjects themselves.

Protect Your Kids: Keeping Children Away from Adult Sites

Wed May 16, 2012 1:32 pm

Protect Your Kids: Keeping Children Away from Adult Sites

In our on-going efforts at Adult FriendFinder to make your experience as fun and safe as possible, we have created this document to help parents understand how to protect their children from inappropriate online material.

The first step to protect your family is to install parental control software on your computer. Some of the best-known and respected parental control software packages are CyberPatrol, Net Nanny and Safety Surf.

Also, some ISPs (Internet Service Providers, the companies that let your modem connect to the Internet) provide content filtering as part of their basic service. Check with your ISP to see if this is an option they offer.

Parental control software works by blocking access to specific websites and online content. In most cases, when you buy the software it already contains a large list of sites that are inappropriate for children. You can then update the software through the manufacturer's website or, in some cases, the software will update itself.

Another way filtering software works is to block sites based on key words, such as "sex." However, filtering software doesn't have to just block access to adult-oriented material. You can configure the software to filter for topics such as tobacco, drugs and drug culture, alcohol, violence and racism.

Since there might be only one computer in your household, and you might be using the same computer as the children, you can set up the system to filter content during certain hours, such as when you're at work and not around to supervise your children's web surfing. You can also setup the system to create a password, that only you know, to override the restrictions.

Some programs can also block personal information, such as name, address and phone number, from being sent from your computer. This is an excellent way to protect children from potential online predators.

Many programs allow you to create different levels of security and filtering based on the different ages of the computer's users. Children can be given high security and heavy content filtering, but when you log on to the machine, you can set it to not filter any content at all.

One thing to remember is that by installing filtering software on your computer, you might also restrict children's' access to legitimate sites. This is especially true if you rely on key words (such as "sex") for blocking. Certain key words appear on legitimate news and information sites, so it's best to experiment with different settings when configuring the filter controls.

Installing filtering software is no guarantee that children won't be exposed to some inappropriate material online. New websites pop up everyday, so it's important to keep your software up to date. Also, learn how your Internet browser software works so that you can check the sites your family has visited (this is the "History" feature, which displays a list of websites visited by the web browser).

Talking to your children about the possible dangers that exist on the Internet, and supervising their web surfing are still the best ways to protect them.

Some key general Internet-related safety points for your children:

Tell them to never give out personal information about themselves or the family to strangers they might meet online or in a chat room.

Remind them that online it's easy for people to pretend to be someone else. They can easily change their name, age and gender in an effort to get close to children.

Teach them that they should never meet a new online friend without an adult present.

Tell them to never give out their picture to a stranger, and that if they ever get a picture with sexual content, or something they find disturbing, that they should get off the computer immediately and tell you about it.

Let them know that if they encounter something or someone dangerous that they can tell you about it, and that you won't blame them or get mad.

Here are some sites where you can get parental control software:

CyberPatrol

http://www.cyberpatrol.com/

Safety Surf

http://www.safetysurf.com/

The Liberal

Mon May 14, 2012 4:39 pm

Editor's Note: Much of Dr. Baker's original description of sociopolitical character types referred to the ideological beliefs of those types. Many of these ideological beliefs have changed in the 45 years since Baker wrote. What has not changed are the specific characterological traits which one observes in the different sociopolitical characters, which Baker describes beautifully in the excerpt below. [Robert A. Harman, M.D., Reprinted from The Journal of Orgonomy, volume 35, number 1]

The term "Modern Liberal" needs clarification as it has become rather misleading with shifts in the current political discourse. Currently, the more accurate and descriptively precise term "Pseudo-Liberal" has replaced it. We have retained the original here for historic purposes.

The True Liberal

The [true] liberal is generally a verbal type, optimistic, intelligent, and prone to intellectualism. He is outwardly sophisticated, emotionally superficial. The energy concentrated in the head gives him buoyancy and general lightness, having nothing to do with actual weight; his feet are not quite on the ground. He is prone to anxiety and concomitant impatience. His outlook is mechanistic so he usually likes urban life. His acute intellect often makes him sensitive and perceptive, but intellectualization also prevents great depth of feeling. His emphasis is as much on style as on content. Violence is abhorrent to him, aggression disturbs him; he would not choose a career in the military, police, or FBI. The true liberal's concentration of energy in the brain allows for fuller development of mental talents, but at the expense of contact with his core. His values are thus less in keeping with nature, more superficial. Thus his character is less stable than the conservative's and more prone to degenerate into exaggeration and destructive social attitudes.

Socially, the [true] liberal is a moderate who stands, both rationally and out of guilt, for extensive improvement for the lot of the common man. Pushed to impatience by anxiety, and disillusioned with the slowness and inefficiency of social progress, he calls upon a central government to innovate and force changes. Believing in the common man and identified with him, he is sure he will respond to these changes by assuming the necessary responsibility to handle them. He calls for more education, an easing of moral restrictions, and less repressive religions, all of which are unquestionably commendable goals. Having maintained some contact with his core, he has feeling, but his intellect is dominant in trying to solve the problems of humanity. He does not understand the structure of man, with its sexual repression and guilt, and cannot see that this structure will not allow man to respond to freedom, nor to accept it. Thus bewildered, the [true] liberal believes that ever more and more change is necessary, so he must continue his Herculean task forever onward. His outlook is constructive, but hampered by insufficient insight and by his own guilt and anxiety. Certainly, he effects much good, and when his ideas are well balanced with the conservative philosophy, the result is a very satisfactory solution to social progress.

The true liberal is open to reason and facts, is accessible and naturally polite. He can openly show his disturbance at facts and reasons that shake his prior beliefs and is capable of change. If he becomes emotional, he may express appropriate anger at abuses or frustrations, but he never becomes hysterically derisive like the modern liberal, because he has no need to defend his beliefs by a dogma. His liberalism seldom comes up as an issue in therapy.

The Modern Liberal

Strictly speaking, although he calls himself one, the modern liberal is not a liberal at all, but a collectivist. He is strongly defended by a dogma and when this is attacked he becomes contemptuous, derisive, and replies with verbal formulas and sarcasm. [Footnote 1] He has an unshakable, unrealistic conviction of his own infallibility and intellectual superiority.... Although modern liberals are actually few in number compared to true liberals or environmental liberals, their influence is felt out of proportion to their number because their anxiety presses them to force acceptance of their needs and since, by nature, they are clever, vociferous, and exceptionally articulate. They are the policymakers behind the scenes in government or the writers of articles of opinion in intellectual magazines and other media of communication. It is because their dangerous ability to influence the thinking of people not only in this country but throughout the world is so great at the present time that I devote so much time to a description of their character structure. Nietzsche has described [the] modern liberal as follows: [Footnote 2]

There is a very narrow, imprisoned, enchained sort of thinker who wants approximately the opposite of our intentions and instincts.... They belong, to make it short and sad, among the levelers, these falsely named "free-thinkers." They are glib-tongued and scribble-mad slaves of democratic taste and its "modern ideas"; all of them are men without solitude, without solitude of their own; what they would like to strive for with all their power is the universal green pasture-happiness of the herd: security, lack of danger, comfort and alleviation of life for everyone. Their most frequently repeated songs and doctrines are "equal rights" and "compassion for all that suffers." Suffering is taken by them as something that must be abolished.

Characterologically this liberalism represents a misfired solution to the problem of guilt and anxiety: the anxiety gets bound up in political attitudes and ties, fixed to a specific and characteristic ideology. These "self-evident" truths the modern liberal sees as unshakable and unarguable, since any attempt to challenge them shakes the very core of his defenses and stirs up intolerable anxiety. The modern liberal ... is further from genital primacy [than the true liberal] and less capable of

111

rational functioning. He expounds all the ideas of the true liberal, not any longer for their own sake, but because they give him the feeling of righteousness and purpose. His humanitarianism is largely rationalization. His concern for others is not at all sincere, as in reality he is quite venomous, and his sympathy for the underdog is merely a reaction formation. The modern liberal lives almost entirely in his intellect. His brain is his substitute for genital potency; it gives him a basis for feeling superior, much as the phallic character uses his erect penis to feel superior. The [modern] liberal pierces everyone around him with his sharp brain. In place of phallic contempt, the [modern] liberal uses intellectual contempt, arrogance, and clever verbal castration. His wit is barbed, amusing at the expense of others. He is void of kind or gentle feelings, except superficially in his causes, and that of course stops all argument, since anyone who "feels so deeply" about the injustices of the world must be above reproach.

This intellectualism is his chief defense against feeling, especially his guilt and anxiety which color and pervade all his attitudes. His anxiety makes immediate fulfillment of his needs imperative, so he tends to favor revolutionary rather than evolutionary tactics. Since his real problem lies elsewhere, he is never satisfied, but needs to advocate constant change and expediency rather than long-range goals. Behind his guilt lies the unresolved Oedipal conflict with the father, whom he fears. Characteristically, he is secretly rebellious against the father whereas the conservative is openly competitive. [Footnote 3] Because he cannot compete with the father, he hates both the competition and the father and identifies always with the underdog, the unsuccessful and the indolent. Subversively defiant, he dares not show any open aggression, so great is the fear of the father and so intense the guilt. Moreover, his bio system cannot stand it. He can allow himself to be aggressive only in causes and abstractions. Any other aggression fills him with intense anxiety and leads him to pacify, compromise, appease. For this reason, he is unable to assume responsible leadership whether it be in government or in raising a child. Privilege he wants as a right and not something that must be earned competitively.

The liberal's intellectualism, guilt, and fear of the father leads directly to his egalitarianism. He feels guilt at his own success or advantages and is thus opposed to differences in social structure. Basically, he needs to feel that all people are the same. They are brothers and should fraternize freely. Because of his anxiety he cannot wait for evolutionary change and therefore advocates governmental social and economic planning, at a federal rather than local level. He wants the government to remove all differences among people (leveling). From this he gets a sense of belonging which dilutes his guilt. No one (the father) is better than he, no one (the criminal) is worse....

In his secret rebellion against the father he identifies with the underdog. An extreme form of this is his sympathetic indulgence of the criminal with whom he identifies through guilt. [Footnote 4] This indulgence of the criminal the [modern] liberal calls his "enlightened" or "modern" attitude of "understanding" the criminal. Punishing the criminal activates his own guilt and interferes with his ability to suppress criminality and juvenile delinquency. The criminal, the delinquent, and the law-abiding citizen all become "equal." At the same time, liberals view the entire military with contempt, as they do the police, because (1) their purpose is to protect society, not rebel against it, and (2) these are not intellectual careers but active, aggressive ones, and what the [modern] liberal cannot accept, he derides. This is of course, an emotional plague reaction. That the military and police provide for his personal safety and well-being, and this at great peril to themselves, evokes no feeling of gratitude or admiration.

The [modern] liberal's need to identify with the underdog is most passionately expressed in his stand on the racial question. In this, as in all his causes, the [modern] liberal is hysterically impatient.... He tries to correct social wrongs by legislation, but the real problem goes back to biophysical readiness, which means responsibility. This requires change of structure, reorientation, and education, through gradual rather than sudden processes, for both Negroes and whites. Because the [modern] liberal has little feeling for true responsibility, he also ignores the Negroes' share of responsibility for their behavior and situation in life. [Footnote 5] He rationalizes and excuses Negro lawlessness and rioting as expected behavior from their long suppression....

Many injustices are committed on the altar of social consciousness.... I do not mean to imply that a sense of social justice is pathological. One has to look at the source. In the [modern] liberal the express motives are not the real motives. There is a great difference between a stock altruism based on hidden guilt and a genuine feeling for the golden rule, reality based. This stock altruism is not open to argument, because the [modern] liberal does not argue rationally, rather he uses sarcasm to imply that any intelligent and reasonable person would think as he does. He supports his premise by rhetoric rather than logic. [Footnote 6] He mentions reason often in his arguments-and even enthrones it as a panacea [Footnote 7] but seldom is he open to it.

Through his intellectualization he has withdrawn energy from his pelvis. He has largely or wholly lost contact with his core, that is, with his natural feelings, and substituted a superficial social facade of concern for all mankind. He likes to think of himself as a world citizen and has contempt for nationalism, a defensive repudiation of his country (father) and its success. His concern for the peoples of the world is purely verbal, especially in those who approach the extreme left of the spectrum.... It is also a reactive defense against his real contempt for people. He has no loyalty to home, community, or country.

His intellectualism makes the modern liberal mechanistic rather than mystical. Religion is taken lightly if not discarded altogether for a purely mechanistic philosophy or dialectic. Having no recourse to religion to solve or handle his guilt, he is driven relentlessly to solve all problems of humanity with an overpowering immediacy, regardless of the rationality of his means or solutions.... He thus advocates with firm conviction the efficacy of the "universal dialogue." He does not say discussion and this is interesting and correct. He does not believe in discussion but merely in words. He talks and writes voluminously but never gets to the point. [Footnote 8]

Sex, like religion, the [modern] liberal also takes lightly. As supporter of "modern" sex concepts, he calls for sexual freedom, as he does for all other freedoms, but does not want the responsibility that goes with it. Thus, what he really supports is license and promiscuity. [Footnote 9] Cut off from real feeling, he writes books on sex-glib, unrestrained, and irresponsible as to what they urge on the public. He misleadingly depicts "different kinds of orgasm," that is, pregenital orgasms in adults, as the goal of genital union and is totally ignorant of the nature and function of genital orgasm. He equates fornication with genuine sexual love or else denies that sex and love have any connection. His excessive concern over the minutest details of pregenital play, his mechanical and studied approach, are in direct proportion to his personal orgasmic frustration and impotence....

Another facet of the [modern] liberal approach, particularly in keeping with his intellectualism, is in his promotion of progressive education. This is a misinterpretation and distortion of the teachings of the liberal philosopher and educator John Dewey and his followers. The emphasis is placed on social adjustment, group activities, group thinking, and social studies rather than on learning per se. Discipline is given minimal consideration if any, and students are promoted automatically regardless of marks. Competition is considered bad for the child, and it is felt that examinations should be eliminated. Since World War II there has been a trend orienting the child toward thinking of himself as a world citizen, downgrading patriotism, loyalty to country, and respect for America's past heroes.

Or, the modern liberal may attempt to follow the teachings of A. S. Neill of Summerhill. He claims to be "on the side of the child" but fails to understand either Neill or the child. [Footnote 10] The result is a guilt-distorted, mechanical application of "freedom-oriented" and "sex-affirmative" techniques in which "all the right things" are rammed down the child's throat, creating confusion, resentment, frustration, brattiness, beatnikism. What is ignored is the child's emotional capacity to accept such teachings or to assume the responsibility for their correct application....

The liberal does not set out specifically to foster communism, he sets out only to protect his own defenses. Yet liberalism is every day steering civilization toward communism and away from free-flowing life. In becoming emancipated from old repressions and restrictions, the human being must be that much more adequate and capable of accepting the greater responsibility which goes with greater freedom. Never having understood himself and his feelings, however, and never having been capable of behaving rationally, he was not prepared for any new freedom. He has reacted to it by increased fear of life, and, as a result, by trying to reduce the size of life to the size of his own brain. Every day contact with himself and his true feelings becomes that much more difficult and that much more to be feared. In his effort to keep control, he has become not only more irrational, like the ordinary neurotic, but has moved increasingly toward controlling other people, like the emotional plague. Total mechanistic control over everyone is what communism is, and as the liberal moves steadily and quickly to the left, the point will occur where liberalism turns into communism. The process is evident in the fact that the [modern] liberal is today less interested in opposing communism than in opposing conservatism. The [modern] liberal considers that the enemy is to the right; communism is "not so bad." [Footnote 11] In place of the old self-control imposed by repression and taboos, there is now to be the "improvement" of mass control by bureaucracy. In place of a sex-negative attitude imposed upon a basically healthy feeling of life, there is now to be sexual "freedom" with the loss of the capacity for love. The latter is by far more life-negating. Contact with nature has been given up, without which man has no feeling of belonging, no real home, without which life is no longer life but only a worthless imitation.

It is this core of total devitalization in the [modern] liberal which is responsible for his attitude of "peace at any price." Functionally, to be at peace is to be bioenergetically unblocked, to flow and stream, consonant with a deep, inner feeling of well-being. That is, there is no such thing as peace without true inner freedom. Those whose devotion to peace is real know full well that there is a time for tranquility and a time for fighting.... The pacifistic liberal of today is seeking rather to arrange his environment so that there is the least disturbance to his crippled energy system. His assumption that the communistic plague can be appeased, educated by example, or blackmailed by world opinion is, from the functional energetic viewpoint, an untenable illusion. It is an acute political myopia; he cannot look clearly at the political situation because it is a product of his own structure, which he cannot afford to view objectively. The pacifist is using his intellect to rationalize his real motive, which is fear of genuine movement. He can propose only one solution. Talk. But no matter how prolific or eloquent he is with words...behind the liberal exhortation is a crippled energy system which cannot tolerate movement or healthy aggression.

The modern liberal is contemptuous of capitalism. The expressed reason is that capitalism is cruel and heartless: the real reason is that capitalism is cruel to him, because it is a system in which individuals must compete on their own, which he cannot tolerate...[Thus the modern liberal advocates that the government interfere in the constructive work of others]. The expressed motive is to help those unable to succeed; the real motive is to eliminate success, so that he will not have to feel anxious and inferior. [Footnote 12] Otherwise said, his wish is to castrate the successful (father) and to eliminate the means by which people become successful (what might be called castration of the nation, i.e. the fatherland). The stated motive is never the real one, which is why I call his rebellion subversive. The [modern] liberal's opposition to all differences in social structure, is, likewise, an expression of his need to pull down the mighty (father)....

Reich has given the clue to the bioenergetic nature of liberalism. He states, "In the ethical and social ideals of liberalism we recognize the representation of the superficial layer of the character, self-control and tolerance. The ethics of this liberalism serve to keep down the 'beast' in man, the second layer, our secondary impulses, the Freudian 'unconscious.' The natural sociality of the deepest nuclear layer is alien to the liberal. He deplores the perversion of human character and fights

116

it with ethical norms, but the social catastrophes of this century show the inadequacy of this approach." [Footnote 13]

The liberal, thus, is ever in the position of defending himself against a breakdown into secondary impulses. He organizes his life and his thinking (his intellectuality) in the service of his defense. His fear of aggression is rooted in the fear of a collapse of his defenses that might result from an energic push, particularly if the aggression is directed against something that would expose the nature of his character. He cannot tolerate movement and tries to avoid excitation of his bio system. From this may be derived the ideas concerning adjustment, equality, peace, etc. This is the character type who swells the ranks of the so-called peace movements, civil rights groups, and "friendship with the enemy" societies. Their frequent show of anti-American feelings, whether open or disguised, is a reaction against the amount of healthy aggression still prevalent in American institutions. It is also a reflection of their unresolved Oedipal situation of rebellion against the father, a rebellion that is always subversive, never open (the role of Oedipal guilt is discussed above under "Characteristics and Symptoms"). They magnify and dramatize a basically rational fear of atomic disaster as a projection of their own personal fear of bioenergetic disintegration. They use their intellectual resources and media to create a mass hysteria that is paralyzing to a defense effort. They are more willing to see the necessity of direct action against a Nazi threat than against communists, since an exposure of the communists is a partial exposure of themselves.

As noted above, the use of intellect as a defense is particularly characteristic. Reich has suggested that the brain may have become so large and complex that it acts essentially as a parasite, sucking up energy from the body, particularly from the pelvis. This may account for the frequent eye block problem of intellectuals and the so-called "intellectual look" of the "egghead." In fact loss of contact by withdrawal or blocking in the eyes is, I believe, a prerequisite for the use of intellectualism as a defense. The resulting fear of disintegration explains the inordinate need among liberal types to "belong." They find in the mass protest groups of society the support, compensatory aggression, and extra strength for their defenses as well as revenge against their alleged tormentors. They tend to be either hysterically energetic or passively intellectual (superior). Neither type of expression is of course indicative of natural healthy energy regulation or genitality. They are quick to support any group which provides them safely with the belonging, revenge, and defenses they seek -- to fill the gap between their longings and their poor capacity for fulfillment. They have lost contact with their core and must defend themselves from any impulses that come from it. Communism represents an even more desperate flight and may be said to be mankind's most desperate flight from itself in history. In communism, man flees from unattainable god within himself (the bioenergetic core) and from historical theism which he rejects intellectually and cannot tolerate emotionally -- to the attainable and tolerable illusion of God to which in final desperation he surrenders with complete faith everything that is basically human.

The Environmental Liberal

I wish to clarify one type of liberal that seems paradoxical in this context. This is what I call the environmental liberal. Actually he is structurally not a liberal at all but is a conservative with liberal ideas. He is anti-communist, moderate in his views, and sincere and one can sense his conservative structure almost immediately.... He grew up in a liberal environment but liberalism never became a part of his structure. It is therefore easily given up. This type of liberal remains open to education and facts, but albeit is rather naïve to political persuasion. He probably constitutes the greatest number of liberals.

Footnotes

1. For an excellent exposition of modern liberalism as an elaborate system of dogma read, James Burnham, Suicide of the West (New York, Day, 1964).

2. From Beyond Good and Evil, Friedrich Nietzsche, H. Regnery Co., Chicago, 1955, paragraph 44.

3. Although this is literally true in many cases it is meant rather as an expression of rebellion against the father image or heritage. The same is true in the case of the conservative's identification with the father.

4. In a letter to the New York Times, October 4,1964, Daniel Gutman, Dean of the New York Law School and former President Justice of the Municipal Court of the City of New York, said in part: "Every day in the week lawyers engaged in defending criminals argue that it is better for '100' or '500' or '1000' guilty men to go free than have one innocent

person punished. This interpretation of the ancient biblical axiom means that it is better to let loose an army of inhuman felons on society than to risk erroneous conviction of an innocent person. The possibility of error cannot be entirely eradicated.... We are virtually encouraging criminals.... Every safeguard must be provided to protect the innocent [but] every proper means should be invoked to enable us to combat...the evil, destructive acts of the wanton criminal.... In many of these cases where the convictions have not been permitted to stand, the guilt of the accused has been established beyond any doubt."

5. A Negro clergyman in Harlem, Bishop James P. Roberts, had the courage to say of conditions there, "Instead of hurting the children and talking of bussing, let's get down to the main trouble in Harlem schools, the indifference of the Negro parents and the lawlessness of their children.... But first we must show that we can be responsible in our own community; this is not a question of poverty but one of morality." New York Times, February 14, 1964. A few other Negro leaders have similarly pointed out the need for responsibility. This is not a modern liberal attitude. The Interfaith Health Association in Queens, Long Island is another good example of responsibility in the community. This association has already won a small victory in eliminating both slum and slum psychology and at the same time promoted true integration rather than a paternalistic one.

6. Cf. Sydney Hook's discussion of the ritualistic liberal who relies on rhetoric rather than logic, slogans rather than analysis of problems. Political Power and Personal Freedom (New York, Criterion Books, Inc., 1959).

7. Just as the French revolutionaries proclaimed, "The Age of Reason."

8. Editor's Note: Both the true liberal and the modern liberal have difficulty getting to the point. However, the modern liberal uses talk not only to avoid getting to the point himself, but, more importantly, to interfere with the capacity of others to think clearly. The presence of a modern liberal often creates a chaotic situation where no one is allowed to get to the point. [Robert A. Harman, M.D.]

9. One can understand his interest in pornography, which is essentially an intellectualized sexual outlet. He frequently calls this art.

10. This does not apply to all schools that follow Neill. The Fifteenth Street School in New York City, for example, [was] seriously interested in the welfare of the child and [had] a true understanding of freedom.

11. Malcolm Muggeridge, British critic, in his review of The Liberal Establishment, by M. Stanton Evans in Esquire, September 1965, makes the following statement: "We liberals are so made that...anyone foolish enough to be on our side is a villain. We despise a Tshombe who, by and large, would seem to be well disposed toward us, and venerate a Nkrumah, who hates our guts and never hesitates to say so.... Liberalism will be seen historically as the great destructive force of our time; much more so than communism, fascism, Nazism or any of the other lunatic creeds which make such immediate havoc.... As mankind goes to their last incinerated extinction, the voice of the liberal will be heard proclaiming the realization at last of life, liberty, and the pursuit of happiness."

12. Editor's Note: This is true even in cases where the modern liberal individual experiences lasting fame, material wealth, etc. It is no exaggeration to say that lack of core contact and absence of constructive achievement render the modern liberal eternally insecure.

13. The Mass Psychology of Fascism, Preface to the Third Edition (New York, Orgone Institute Press, 1946), p. viii.

BIRD-WATCHING CAN HELP BOOST ECOTOURISM INDUSTRY

Sun May 13, 2012 2:21 pm

New York, May 10 2012 5:10PM

Bird-watching, a popular hobby around the world, can present significant economic opportunities for countries through sustainable tourism, the United Nations environment agency said today, stressing that States should increase efforts to support this growing industry.
"Birding plays a significant and growing part in the tourism industry, and creates direct and indirect economic benefits for many countries and

communities, also amongst developing countries," said the Acting Executive Secretary of the Convention on the Conservation of Migratory Species of Wild Animals (CMS), Elizabeth Maruma Mrema, in a <"http://www.cms.int/news/PRESS/nwPR2012/pressreleases/wmbd_10 0512_e.pdf">news release ahead of World Migratory Bird Day, which is observed on 12-13 May.

Initiated in 2006, the Day is an annual campaign organized by CMS and the African-Eurasian Migratory Waterbird Agreement (AEWA) – two intergovernmental wildlife treaties administered by the UN Environment Programme (UNEP), which also backs the campaign – and devoted to celebrating migratory birds and promoting their conservation worldwide.

In a news release, UNEP highlighted that global spending on all areas of ecotourism is increasing by about six times the industry-wide rate of growth, and underlined the potential economic benefits of bird-watching in particular.

In the United States, for example, a survey by authorities puts the economic value generated every year by bird and other wildlife watchers at around $32 billion in that country alone. This amount corresponds to the gross domestic product of Costa Rica, which is also a popular destination for US birdwatchers.

In Scotland, the Royal Society for the Protection of Birds found that last year, between $8-12 million is spent annually by tourists wishing to see White-tailed Eagles on the Isle of Mull alone, and that four per cent of jobs in Scotland are associated with wildlife tourism.

World Migratory Bird Day seeks to spotlight these benefits while also raising awareness of the importance of protecting birds, which face a series of challenges each year in their journeys.

"Conserving migratory birds is highly challenging because their annual migration often spans several countries, each governed by its own jurisdiction and national conservation strategies," Ms. Mrema said.

Events to mark the Day are due to take place in 70 countries, including bird festivals, education programs, presentations, film screenings and bird watching trips, run by hundreds of volunteers and organizations.

The Day will be followed by an AEWA intergovernmental conference on migratory waterbirds, which will take place on 14-18 May in La Rochelle, France, and will focus on the role that wetlands play as a vital habitat for migratory birds and people and as a source of livelihoods for communities, particularly in Africa.

"It is absolutely critical that governments use the forthcoming meeting, to continue to do all they can to work together to try to safeguard, retain and where feasible restore high quality habitats – and to begin to link the conservation of migratory birds to human development and livelihoods on a flyway scale," said the Acting Executive Secretary of AEWA, Marco Barbieri.

Beethoven

Fri May 11, 2012 5:25 pm

The fact that Beethoven got def, I could first trace the situation on the 13th century where the crusades took place. In between in the Napoleon invasions (19th century) and with the religious wars, the composer, one century before, felt the outcome of poetry by his ears so delicate and he made beautiful music with his def condition. His: Poets are never young, in one sense. Their delicate ear hears the Far-off whispers of eternity, which coarser souls must travel towards For scores of years.

History of the Archives of the Orgone Institute

Fri May 11, 2012 11:36 am

On March 8, 1957, four days before he was taken to a federal prison, Wilhelm Reich signed his Last Will & Testament. By this time his orgone energy accumulators and many of his publications had already been banned and destroyed by order of a United States Federal Court injunction, starting on June 5, 1956 when three orgone energy accumulators were destroyed outside of Reich's Student Laboratory at Orgonon in Rangeley, Maine.
Three weeks later, several boxes of his publications were burned under the supervision of Food and Drug Administration agents outside the Student Laboratory. A month after that, in July, the panels for about fifty orgone accumulators were dismantled in the town of Rangeley, Maine by the local contractors who had built them.
And exactly one month after that—on August 23, 1956—several tons of Reich's publications, including the titles of 10 hardcover books as well as medical and scientific research bulletins and journals, were burned under

FDA supervision at a New York City municipal garbage incinerator on Gansevoort Street.

All of which undoubtedly weighed heavily on Reich on March 8, 1957, four days before he would begin a two-year prison sentence for criminal contempt of court. In the opening paragraph of his Last Will and Testament, Reich wrote:

"I made the consideration of secure transmission to future generations of a vast empire of scientific accomplishments the guide in my last dispositions. To my mind, the foremost task to be fulfilled was to safeguard the truth about my life and work against distortion and slander after my death."

And to accomplish this task, in his will he created a Trust, originally known as the Wilhelm Reich Infant Trust Fund. This Trust was so-named because of Reich's belief that the only real solution to eliminating psychological disturbances and their subsequent somatic illnesses was prevention, and that this prevention was possible only by ensuring what he called "the unspoiled protoplasm" and the "unarmored life" of infants who he called "The Children of the Future."

Thus, on March 8, 1957, Reich's concerns and his practical solutions for transmitting his legacy to future generations after his death, culminated in the signing of this Last Will & Testament.

Four days later–on March 12, 1957–Reich entered the Federal Penitentiary in Danbury, Connecticut. Ten days after that–on March 22nd, two days before his 60th birthday–Reich was transferred to the Federal Penitentiary in Lewisburg, Pennsylvania to serve his two-year sentence. Seven-and-a-half months later–on November 3, 1957–he died in the Lewisburg Penitentiary of heart failure and was buried several days later at Orgonon.

In his Last Will & Testament, Reich had named his daughter, Dr. Eva Reich, as the sole Trustee of The Wilhelm Reich Infant Trust Fund. She was the individual now charged with carrying out Reich's final wishes as stipulated in his will. And among the will's principal stipulations was this: "To operate and maintain the property at Orgonon under the name and style of The Wilhelm Reich Museum."

In the will, Reich elaborated on this stipulation, by enumerating some specific responsibilities. He says:

"I have collected all of the pertinent materials, such as instruments which served the Discovery of the Life Energy, the documents which were witnesses to labors of some 30 years the library of a few thousand volumes, collected painstakingly over the same stretch of time, and amply used in my researches and writings.

"All of these things and similar things should remain where they are now to preserve some of the atmosphere in which the Discovery of the Life Energy has taken place over the decades. The grounds should be kept neat and clean, and repairs should not be neglected."

Well before his imprisonment, Reich had stored his archives in two separate locations in one building:

In a photographic dark-room on the first floor of the Orgone Energy Observatory, which is the major building at Orgonon, and is now the Museum.

And in a large closet off of Reich's study and library on the second floor of the Observatory.

And in his will, immediately after his stipulations about the Museum, Reich begins his discussion about his archives:

"In order to enable the future student of the Primordial Cosmic Energy Ocean, the Life Energy discovered and developed by me, to obtain a true picture of my accomplishments, mistakes, wrong assumptions, pioneering basic trends, my private life, my childhood, etc., I hereby direct that under no circumstances and under no pretext whatsoever shall any of the documents, manuscripts or diaries found in my library among the archives, or anywhere else, be altered, omitted, destroyed, added to, or falsified in any other imaginable way. The tendency of man, born from fear, to 'get along with his fellow man' at any price, and to hide unpleasant matters is overpoweringly strong.

"To guard against this trend, disastrous to historical truth, my study including the library and archives, shall be sealed right after my death by the proper legal authorities and no one shall be permitted to look into my papers until my Trustee, hereinafter-named, is duly-appointed and qualified and takes control and custody thereof.

"These documents are of crucial importance to the future of newborn generations. I therefore direct my Trustee and his successors that nothing whatsoever must be changed in any of the documents and that they should be put away and stored for 50 years to secure their safety from destruction and falsification by anyone interested in the falsification and destruction of historical truth."

What is heartbreaking about Reich's will is his implicit hope that his daughter—with the support of his colleagues and students, and with everyone fueled by a singular vision and resolve—would work together to carry out his final wishes regarding the transmission of his legacy to future generations.

And in that hope Reich was completely mistaken.

Regrettably and understandably, Eva Reich was so emotionally devastated by the tragedy of her father's death that months later she let it be known that she didn't feel she could assume the awesome responsibilities of the Trusteeship, that someone else had to be found to do this.

Yet no one among Reich's colleagues and students stepped forward to assume the mantle of the Trusteeship and carry out the specifics of Reich's Last Will & Testament. No cohesive group ever assembled after Reich's death to categorically insure the fulfillment of his final wishes, and not someone else's.

That task ultimately fell to a woman, barely 34 years old—a former patient of Dr. Chester Raphael's—a woman who was unwilling to see Reich's historical legacy possibly lost forever and who stepped forward to offer her services.

That woman was Mary Boyd Higgins.

In the early 1959, during the winter, Mary traveled to rural Rangeley, Maine to visit Reich's over 200-acre property at Orgonon for the first time. The Student Laboratory and the Orgone Energy Observatory were abandoned, boarded up and vandalized, unattended and unprotected for nearly two years against the harsh New England elements.

Inside the Orgone Energy Observatory, Wilhelm Reich's archives were gone: removed illegally the previous year by Aurora Karrer, the last woman in Reich's life, who had transported the archives hundreds of miles away to the house that she shared with her mother in Bethesda, Maryland.

And to make matters worse, when Reich's Last Will & Testament was finally probated and all specific personal bequests were fulfilled, $823 was all that was left for Mary Higgins to turn this situation around and carry out Reich's final wishes.

Today, that would translate into approximately $5,800. Less than $6000 to transform Orgonon from the ruin that it was into the beautiful and vibrant property and museum that it is today. Less than $6000 to retrieve and protect Reich's archives for future generations, according to the dictates of his will.

Shortly after that first visit to Orgonon, Mary Higgins traveled to Bethesda, Maryland. And during several face-to-face meetings, Ms. Karrer repeatedly denied that she had these archival materials. Only when Mary Higgins took legal action against her, did Ms. Karrer and her attorney produce suitcase after suitcase after suitcase with these archival materials, which the Court subsequently turned over to the Trust.

But many archival materials were still missing. And the Trust's legal efforts to retrieve additional materials from Ms. Karrer would stretch across over four decades.

In terms of Reich's final wishes to establish a Museum: living in Rangeley was a gentleman by the name of Tom Ross who for years had been the caretaker at Orgonon while Reich was alive. In fact, for a time he and his wife Bea and their daughter Kathy actually lived in one of the cottages at Orgonon (which is now our rental cottage called Bunchberry). The entire Ross family became close friends with Mary Higgins. And with their assistance, their generosity of time and hard physical work, Mary was able to open Orgonon to the public in 1960 as The Wilhelm Reich Museum.

Today, Orgonon comprises 175-acres of fields and forests and trails which are open daily to the public:

The Orgone Energy Observatory–which had been abandoned, boarded up and vandalized–is now listed on the National Register of Historic Places and is open for tours in the summer and early fall, and by special tours.

The Student Laboratory–which had also been abandoned and vandalized–is now the Conference Building and the location of the Museum and Trust offices.

Jumping back now to 1959, the first year of Mary Higgins' tenure as Trustee: a third area of responsibility began to emerge for the Trust, in addition to creating a Museum and safeguarding the archives. That third responsibility was re-publishing Reich's books, although publishing was not a specific stipulation in Reich's Last Will & Testament.

This is the way it happened:

A young scholar named Leo Raditsa–who was interested in Reich's work–approached Roger Straus of Farrar, Straus & Giroux which, at the time, was a flourishing 13-year old New York publishing house. In 1959, there was still considerable interest in Reich's work. But it was difficult or impossible for people to find copies of Reich's books–except maybe in second-hand bookstores–because a 1954 Court Injunction had banned Reich from distributing them and because tons of Reich's books, from his Orgone Institute Press in New York, had been burned in 1956.

Raditsa explained to Straus that perhaps there was an audience for these books. And he wondered if Straus might explore the possibility of bringing them back into print. The result of this was a wonderful and productive 45-year professional relationship between Roger Straus and Mary Higgins, as well as a genuine personal friendship, during which time all of Reich's hardcover books were re-published and several new titles were brought out. Starting in 1960 with the publication of Selected Writings – An Introduction to Orgonomy. The concept of this book was actually Roger Straus's who felt that an anthology of excerpts from Reich's books might be the best way to introduce his work to a broader, more mainstream audience. This was followed by the publication of:

The Function of the Orgasm (1961)

The Sexual Revolution (1962)

Character Analysis (1963)

Listen, Little Man! (1965)

The Murder of Christ (1966)

Reich Speaks of Freud (1967), an entirely new book which was published over the vehement objections of Dr. Kurt Eissler of The Sigmund Freud Archives

The Mass Psychology of Fascism (1969)

The Invasion of Compulsory Sex-Morality (1971)

Ether, God and Devil / Cosmic Superimposition (1973)

The Cancer Biopathy (1973)

Early Writings – Volume One (1975)

People in Trouble (1976)

The Bion Experiments on the Origin of Life (1979)

Genitality – Early Writings, Volume Two (1980), Reich's revision of his 1927 German-language book Die Funktion des Orgasmus

Record of a Friendship: Correspondence of Wilhelm Reich and A.S. Neill (1981)

The Bioelectrical Investigation of Sexuality and Anxiety (1982)

Children of the Future (1983)

Passion of Youth – An Autobiography (1988)

Beyond Psychology – Letters and Journals, 1934-1939 (1994)

American Odyssey – Letters and Journals, 1940-1947 (1999)

At the time of Mr. Straus's death in May 2004 at the age of 87, Farrar, Straus & Giroux had published 21 titles by Reich, including three volumes of his diaries and journals, and the correspondence between Reich and A.S. Neill. And because of the publishing house's strong international presence, Reich's books now appear in over 21 languages.

What is so moving about Mr. Straus's relationship with the Trust is this: he was the first to admit that he had no great personal interest nor understanding of Reich's work, and that his decision to publish Reich's books was because of his sense of outrage and his need to take a principled stance against book-burning in America.

Roger Straus is truly one of the unsung heroes in transmitting Reich's legacy to future generations, first as a publisher, and second as the individual who brought The Wilhelm Reich Infant Trust to the attention of the Countway Library of Medicine at Harvard University, one of the world's premier medical libraries.

For years after Mary Higgins had legally retrieved the bulk of Reich's Archives from Aurora Karrer, she kept these materials at her home in Forest Hills, New York where she lived up until 2001. And during this time, she visited several institutions, looking for a permanent repository for these materials, including the Library of Congress and several university libraries.

Meanwhile, Roger Straus contacted someone that he knew: a man named Richard Wolfe, the Chief Librarian of the "Rare Books and Special Collections" at Harvard's Countway Library. Mr. Wolfe felt that Reich's legacy was an important one and that these archives would be a welcome addition to the library's other collections.

Consequently, in October 1973 an agreement was signed between the

Trust and the Countway whereby Reich's archival materials would be periodically given to the Countway Library over the years, to be stored in their Rare Books and Special Collections with the Trust retaining all copyright title and publishing rights.

Today at the Countway Library, Reich's archives are kept in a temperature-controlled environment in the Rare Books and Special Collections which renamed and is now known as "The Center for the History of Medicine." Reich's archives comprise well over 200 archive boxes of materials. And starting in November 2007–50 years after Reich's death–these archives became accessible to scholars and researchers.

The Trust also disseminates and safeguards the truth about Reich's life and legacy—and about the Trust's activities—through its presentations at Orgonon's summer conferences, at fundraising events, and at the invitation of other organizations.

Source: http://www.wilhelmreichtrust.org/home.html

Protect children from the sun

Mon May 07, 2012 10:35 pm

Children need special attention, since they tend to spend more time outdoors, can burn more easily, and may not be aware of the dangers. Parents and other caregivers should protect children from excess sun exposure by using the steps described above. Older children need to be cautioned about sun exposure as they become more independent. It is important, particularly in parts of the world where it is sunnier, to cover your children as fully as is reasonable. You should develop the habit of using sunscreen on exposed skin for yourself and your children whenever you go outdoors and may be exposed to large amounts of sunlight. If you or your child burns easily, be extra careful to cover up, limit exposure, and apply sunscreen.

Babies younger than 6 months should be kept out of direct sunlight and protected from the sun using hats and protective clothing. Sunscreen may be used on small areas of exposed skin only if adequate clothing and shade are not available.

Poem for the Jeeser Train

Mon May 07, 2012 9:09 pm

Here it comes Alexander and Avenue, they are a view which rises from down below into the unwritten world of the skies and the skies can see this from both views where there is a feeling which signs the figure of Alexander and Avenue under and above the skies. These two beings are thin, they are a melody figure, living out of your space but inside many spaces; they have the majestic will to uncover many fragments of all emotional incomes by holding what is a dream and what is real, though they exist together like humans and all avenues paraded in and out of the skies. That's why sometimes they clean their aura with the best nature way of saying I am the cosmos. Will you dear reader, allow yourself to look within you and inside the questions that makes your soul to have the shape of a double rainbow? The musical feelings from these beings feel with hope the prolific good pore of living, a good breathing stage of discharging the energy based on the character with a sharpened move of the poetical body as the cosmic language is spelled by good things. Alexander can make the sun from his mind which its skull has curled hair and the legs of a knight. He tells to his twin sister, Avenue, to embrace the lonely orphans of this planet and they feed some people with a strong guiding will in order to cover the human and the cosmos with the natural kingdom of a solemn flying and the floating beauty is the time where the orphans have found their sunny day with a sunny smile, even in cloudy days and cold nights, because the warmth came to refresh the spiritual stage of wisdom across all the streets and all the roads where there is light inside the home of our hearts. Olives had kindled light for centuries. Alexander knew well this type of light, while Avenue was appreciating this kind, after many years with neon light. In between all the lights, there is one that never goes out and that is the spirit in the skies as birth of life. Well Alexander and Avenue went out to seek the gain of joy among with their will self of character, like the seventh dream of a teenage heaven with love and wondering stars. All journeys have their poetry, mainly because it concerns life as she is felt in our travelling souls and that is the meaning of an honest sense that is enduring the splinters from so much seeking. The good flying horse, is taking the wonderers into a higher music where these magicians of hope are embracing the refrains in order to appeal to the good movement of the sacred melodies from what it exists on the imagination of children and giving shape to all the rainbows in every playful event where silence is the ascending sublime time in the presence of the beauty with a movement made by the souls at the time where the pieces of the skies are shining on and on. Alexander went with Avenue to wonder and to seek on the world and their inhabitants with great respect for their existence that by good or mean ways, they could learn and present so much later, if there was dignity in the living signs of all the organisms, being mental, as matter, as body with different shapes and wishes. The will self of being inside all that exists lies at different tempos and the organization of ideas in all aspects that is known and unknown lies by setting time to think about them. Even with unfair traits like stealing the voice into the big science of silence but on this case is a cruel fashion and not the decal of the nudity as we know her by giving birth into many feds with few inspiring movements of two things: the moral beauty and the discipline of truth. On this aspect, humans tend to steal in many ways and the work of Alexander became a silent vulture with music as the lifting voice of what was left as legacy from distant generations. This is the work of a guarder which must ascend into the skies with the generous and brave look all around the avenues with the big one, being centered in here as the guiding process of inspiration and never as a manual. Out Space life surely is surprised with human complexity. For example, the biological realm that makes from this specie and his natural function a view over the color of money, a view that cannot enlace the physical reality of a cat that doesn't need to warm up before climbing into a tree, while humans they have to warm up for everything. One plausible conclusion is that life on Earth is sponsored by small blue things that enter into the realm of an exhausted existence and no Carnival can bring the magicians of hope into the danger that was built in by fear. Why? Because, dear reader, there is surely a prudent way of listening an echo splashed with a well input of the voice being introduced to prevent the explosion of routine. With the knowledge of being critical as result of performing what speaks louder within the seasons, if the color of money or if the colorful face of a child that shows herself rebel, meaning that she didn't lost her critical spirit. The meaning of critic is a shortcut to purity. The laces of dark faces can be felt by observing this sick form of absorbing a reasonable idea. A loyal figure leads the letters from lovers and rebels like the white pigeons from the houses of hermits who love as children do. A distant prudence is taken as virtue with hidden truths because all secrets from love bonds need the guarders as ego helmets. The body cannot endure all tasks and loyalty in humans can attract life with great respect with the critic in several roles such as of bad parenting or the hierarchies all over the population when being young or old has myriads of dichotomies and sad ones because institutions are like slime at the fresh feet of the seeker. The naked gender in here is the safe pore of sanity which lies on the accurate fight against fantasy, triviality and the toy lands which are far from having signs of grace. Then it's up to you reader, to awake, read, think and fast on the way to establish the necessary melody around your sunny day which shall be sponsored by signs of vitality whenever the rebel songs enters in the ages of ancient lutes, somewhere where the skies can be visible in the gender of conscious. The necessity of life is the decal of what is untamed but organized by the infinite logic paths of the Universal vivid reality sustained by her immeasurable existence with important living organisms to pay a higher respect. The surveying of dangerous beings is in the hands of the primitive hermits either in cities or in forests like in Thuringia, by organic farmers, in the chain of nature, in the galaxies. All interact with the respect taking emphasis on the justice issues either in fascism, religious nonsense, money media, criminal content of mandatory laws: all these presences are a practice of living but we own her as Adrienne Rich is a Poetess and her words mean to respect life, that's the aim of a spiritual approach as time also approaches the advices from our ego as he his one friendly ally of every time the dust is untamed by a bad organization of interacting. The best answer is to work in a regular basis, making draws on our emotions that are seen in the body, watching the benefits of Orgonomy when she understands her role as guiding processes to liberate all that is mandatory and that concerns the first, the last and the semper of us all. A crucial care lies in the motion of the organization of time according to the natural beauty of something clean and like a dream, belongs to the realm of warm feelings at the time our eyes meet the income of a changing care in our lives and that exists in the inner conquer of a prolific wealth because, dear reader I am still fond of you. There are primitive reasons as safe guarders of dreams but not in the hands of pedagogues that are the social drinkers of the warfare of a pale fear that harass the way minorities have as their inner being and secular heritage are a friendly wisdom. All that can be felt towards the world's shivering by the laughing tale of the enemies of the medicine I am presenting. Alexander was worried with the decadence of people on their troubled paper money heads and had to postpone his childhood that was in care of Avenue as she is a sweet thing to count with. Both were working hard as the motility of societies, were trying to silence the voices which have their sensitive aims in real danger. Minorities everywhere you, dear reader, will know in the fetus of your body, in the banks of the modern canals where an uncertain providing of goods, don't know how life can be felt by the reservoir of a warm, spontaneous human love into the eye contact with the urgent hours of a beneficial future. A lifetime dream lies in accurate decisions with a regular basis of thinking over these facts and what it can be obtained, is so far, the delivering of a good progressive critic by taking the consequences on our egos by giving life signs as a prolific inspiration into the world as we know him. To the justification of this time, the pleasure in all its seriousness with an immanent sense in the whole circle of all bright soft illuminations which are a vital source in our lives, lie in the platform of solid horizons which are the accurate ascension of the sublime we build every time the gentle wind comes in to procrastinate time in what concerns the awareness of life as should be taken in respect and dignity. That's what Alexander felt while he was emerging on sleeping while Avenue was providing the basic warn signs into the magnetic auras that were so far from being graceful and that made stronger the integration from all the creatures in worry to catch the stolen breath on the world which is turning the screws on people's expectations of what could be a pure form of living. Human triumph used to suffice and Alexander and I, enemies of this truth, had the pleasure to infer it with a predisposition on the eventual wolf in the breast from a kindled moon's light where the eyes are in care in the seek and believe as a edifying seed of every human need. Fear is now preparing to go away and you will be on my jacket tonight, dear reader, because the sky is open to be watched from one leaf as a bird knows how to hide and seek around the trees with little ways of belonging to the magnitude of a sweet geography like the one who maintains human hope and the honey shape of it as it should be tasted in our table with great content. Once seen the beauty, once she is well as art of a calm attention where an indigo virtue is a principle of esteem by obtaining her spirit. Love comes along like merit of the origins that compose the zeal in praxis of the double in us and the one among the union is the best harmony within all imperfections. We are the other as flexible example of our perfection by touching and stopping inside the pure repose of beauty. In the plausible awake of life cycles towards the constancy that death is like the fear from the lack of the pure love unity in our lives has the meaning as a continue act of existing. Settling time can and again seed the poetical outcome of the reality of life and death, in short, we can apply the fact that all the radical journalism has its role in the sense that all exists as concern, as feeling and the wrong misrepresentation of life means deaths in many ways of introducing them. You can live with no political bone but you are responsible for a passive voice on the radical acts that mean death and in honor of this escaping, I can only awake and repose on my poetical bones that have the honor in zeal to warn the cycles of existence that a rejuvenation from the psychological deaths can be achieved by sleeping with a virgin or with a child (with no sexual attachment). The gymnophobia (fear of nudity) is an example of death. We can inspire on the mythological figure of Aesculapius for the settling of a moral rejuvenation in all that concerns pureness in positive standards of bringing information and once taken, we can think, learn, extent her into the origins of life as the great design of hope. Coming back to the good of our health and the work upon the majestic skies which are the mirror of the sea and maybe the presence of nudity in its pure life form, as a friend waiting for us to keep smiling under the orange color dawning because the movement is on our shoulders. Birds are much wiser and why? They know freedom and humans never knew this concept, therefore the necessary display of nature to exemplify the simplest aspects of existence that is so imposed by means into an end. I brought this from a morning coffee at a coffee place where the mandatory work brings plagues and had paid to watch the deadly chains of societies just on the last day of the first decade of the 21th century. So where to find hope, shall we wait for how much more decades of mandatory plaguing as pride in it's the best shape of stupidity as hope sponsors this item as a saying. So never say goodbye but listen and learn with the best poetical examples of flying kingdoms as a good lift to the next sidereal time. The spiritual mirror of thought is a well-prepared conviction at every transitory distance from the life we feel, leading a nursery desire in the dance of all cordial feelings that become clear like a moving and caring expression of a delicate plume, whispering a friendly passion towards our love conclusions based on the core of the mighty open nudity of the ego. The refrain of a balanced heart caresses life by generosity and a interposed confinement of it with the good vision in it, is work being managed for a beneficial adoption of the sage. Being recommended for any chain of thought there is a good credit of prolific life narratives as we paint our peer people as lovers. The festive course of daily ascending elaborated shrines, have the affection of everything that is an interval of motion, thought here as a poetical being kept as saving of the working democracy. In magnified difference there are lines of ideas as immaterial devotion on it concerns the genome that in our delicate organisms, are the vital voice of a good and profound regard of a social regeneration. We can attract the edge of our forces with the dressing reality that explains the twin penetration of the humble ally of the drawing plan being made in the distance that has manners of privilege which can be a moral minority seated to remain as silent lovers. The passion inside the origin of profound silent facilities, are a mutual agreement from one being to the other as accepting the merit of uniqueness. We can wish and desire as also not to act in order to use the profound being of flexible splendors around the purity of all infancy of the skies. This is the look of a beneficial movement that rises from silence into the interesting wonders of the Universe. The poetic roar of vast impressions, belong to the speech of freedom in consensual recollections without authority towards the other. This position is a solemn motion as persuasion into an open and sufficed chapter of life being dressed in practical places where we dare to fit in respect. Then the living was sleeping, hollow was the crying and the emerging talent from the warm ways from nostalgia into the consensual future along the world's best virtue whereas they can send their eyes in here as a visual recognition of all of us in struggle. Alexander and Avenue made a Poem for the Jeeser train,

As I lay on the wooden bed On the top of a thousand books I smoke and think The hermit is working I am in my peace Suddenly the train arrives It whistles and my thinking whereas it's there I take time to think about this train About the driver and the ticket woman I wait and sustain their thoughts on me Then they depart And I whisper them into my thoughts Oh what a wonderful morning train!

The Reservoir from A Six Bell Chime

Mon May 07, 2012 3:50 pm

Dear face beyond emptiness your eyes are gentleness, I am up to high in my dream and you painted so well my primal scream that I will leave you these words as a handshake. May we endure the poetry of love and ache with the random fragility in motion around here, where the salted geography is felt like our tear. Indoors with a long turbulence I stand around the seeking.

CHAPTER I

A DELICATE PASSION AROUND THE PURE LIFE

The way a walk can be a chain of lust getting out somewhere into deepness when our noble care is a trust with the feelings are beyond the taking which we had hold with the necessary display of the body being told about twisting moods and across the skies. Why I all always focus to notice the end of this fly like coming back to my solemn kingdom and it seems too much but not from my reservoir of freedom that keeps breathing as a good company.

Dear face beyond emptiness your eyes are gentleness, I am up to high in my dream and you painted so well my primal scream that I will leave you these words as a handshake. May we endure the poetry of love and ache with the random fragility in motion around here, where the salted geography is felt like our tear. Indoors with a long turbulence I stand around the seeking. Does the insight of a scarlet dream enlarge the being where a calm passion takes hold of this way of tracking the skies? It is just when the sunlight that walks towards the vision upon my eyes and together we can ship the moon by hanging the spin of a cloud. Maybe inside this substance and taking proud in this walk, then the love and the tact are as prudent as the frank arctic. Are you the voice at the seaside, a friendly murmur in deluxe pride which sails with the bird's gentle morphology over the San Elmo's fire? Perhaps existence longs for a sober desire. My political space needs to extend my choice as you woke me and spoke in your tender voice and we fade in passing away from narrowed lives. To caress the experienced taste of love bonds in one memory read in profound and as a curious portrait as we seek, tell, wish. The longing choice taking a hidden shadow from the balance in sirens across the bay, to dance with you on the sandy taste of your name, in your sign that tells me to hear your flame, so come sweet shining spirit, we can stand to swear for secrets that wait hand in hand. The thin agility of a tiny bridge in a low voice is like a delicate motion daring to comply with sharpened changes that ease the injuries.

What it hurts in everyone's memory out of a globe in warm circles that we claim? Should I guard this treasure in me? Open the love in your mood of hope and tell me about this, now and with my credence, wondering to go inside your distant soul, in the old boats, the seagulls in the freedom of the whole. I wish to like you and to accept your smile at me in a distant land, stay inside, for a while in my sincere way because I know hearts; they pulse in the virginity of life, on each gender in each cruel absence but there in far graces by parts, a serious rendezvous is waiting and your windy skirt also wonders what is to be felt everywhere, though I declare my breathing spirit to approach what our joy can dare.

The spirits in fight with the heat that always remark the aspects of shores well united to wait for the glowing in the direction of lips and arms. The confessions taken as art of a confined sacred acceptance that hears the alma mater once risen from coldness and as reply from every of these portmanteaus that influences respect in our own reality, then the good work of huge thinkers enable the fair probabilities and we can be familiar with our own resolutions. I can't handle being the odd one out because friends do not want to face their feelings. My own family cannot face what I know they feel. How can I know that I am not dreaming when I am with the essence of unity around the reflex of my logic? Well, I hold the eye contact on my senses, turning the actual alma mater into nothing less than a penniless logic. But the facility of my shoulders endured 3 ferocious policemen and carried into the skies, a brief salvation from an old man. What happened to the meaning of dream in this note? It stands for the motility of this alma mater when there are no bonds to embrace but in respect for logic, came justice, under the eyes of respect, turning the oppression into the liberation of complexity of the human things. If ageism can take respect as a guiding inspiration into the population something that lasts like the moving story of the Portuguese man, José Mestre, ´A Man With No Face´ on the hearts but independently and longing no more for random brief and urgent salvations but globally. Out of the academic insurance, up too high with those immense forms of casualties that lead youth into the perpetual sadness of being taught as History of Universities had told them. But if you ask into any student or teacher, or a PhD a simple wise question, you can note, that the bird of the gentle tree takes the pure wisdom of this solitaire man with a mighty clear vision and sings for these people every morning because he who writes to prepare the legacy of what is important also carries his own moving story and that is the dream inside the logic.

Sometimes there is a composed exasperation of not being understood among the icons that I created from street poetry, spontaneous philosophy, tutor of nursing, Anarchist activism; the conclusion is that like in silence, it lies in all energetic peer sensations if that is possible to hold, that all that is felt among the collective expressions of love, even if they are sponsored by one other way of whispering time, there are friendly events called enigmas and everything around is a search for company on the biological functions that are on the way of the facts as we act in passion around the pure life.

The dimension of a wide extension of fear like the compulsory education is no form of being human in respect. Going out from this sharpened tear, a thick full source of new creations makes notes in here and thinking on what existence is loaded with, in the precise exactitude about what the human race in its destiny, knowing the lane to be with the act sweeping in their solitude, so that the good heart of the human science guards and works to remark this fact. The note in here goes inside as also comes closer and soon our smile will travel into a shore, to hold the sea poetry and whisper her more over. To strain this open attitude so much more on what we do with all the feelings posted in the unknown truths. In the awake of a brave solitude of youth, there are thinkers in high vivid realities that in the play of their nude wisdom mirror that on its horizon, somehow is a calm strength in action as their eyes enlarge with an exact intention for the shape of the known solitude with its own fraction, taken in dialogs down at the seaside when reality and the thinking collide for the late-night swim and we should go in. The clean enhancement for spirituality has feelings in plurality coming from a misty morning in touch with that hermit's mighty ego nudity in rush for the quietness of Earth's time, as truth in a subliminal sense around a mnemonic being in love and the angle on which your ankles are above. So here it goes my paper note on his curled flying destination into the lucidity of the giant freedom that exists in a poetical recreation. A distant prudence in a sufficed northern windy spirit through a long compel of marching waters still beyond the consolation in the whole of this.

To clean the aura, we can do the following:

1. Using your fingers as a comb, comb through the space surrounding your body from head to toe. Clean your hands with running water before and after doing this.

2. Stand under a waterfall or shower.

3. Walking in the rainfall.

4. Run freely and playfully in the wind.

5. Using a single feather or feather whisk make sweeping motions through the space surrounding your body.

6. Smudge the area surrounding your body with the smoke from sage, lavender, and/or sweet grass.

7. Immerse and soak your body in an Epsom salt bath.

Tips:

1. Turkey or owl feathers are especially good feathers to use for sweeping the aura.

2. Take care to do some deep breathing exercises while cleansing your aura to aid in flushing your inner body.

3. Caution: Do not walk in the rain during an electrical storm.

If you feel better in yourself, make some creative tasks, even if it concerns matter, it will help the spirit to be absent from the height of things and the complex become simple in the duration of your time. Choose your time, you must gather time for you and extend him into peaceful events, like a walk on the beach and if you're too shy like me, make it when there are few people and take with you the necessary things that make you feel safe among the crowd. Pretend that you are and you really can be interested on the plants in the dunes and pay no attention directly into people in front of you. Sometimes and mainly men feel like bad when you look deep inside their eyes and they take it as a provocation to manhood. Sit down because we are all free, the seat takes the eyes into the thought and that will help you to embrace nature and the cosmos. Then you are in harmony because you could be yourself without external mimetic behaviors. That is the simple difference between the passion of uniqueness, free from dark institutions and safe on your freedom to the whole of existence with peace after the boiling conclusion of what it makes the galaxy of yourself, be seen by a kind care of humanity.

CHAPTER III

HANGING THE SPIN FROM A GENEROUS CLOUD

To endure a hiding fire from a lusty sky and the biscuits circle for sonatas in your eye where the body of a candy face runs deep, maybe the dressing cello of your lip that crucifies a sound and a speed and you're in my need by the sacred integrity of a random bliss so more and so far, here's my kiss. This little kiss as the first where a tender thirst that came to refrain an orchard where the May scent and his archery, both have a similar architecture to be explained in what you are involved and sustains a kind of archery that forever and blows with me and you make our things in tasty flows.

The assembled heart carried in for secrets as being reverenced out of the counting years, where the gospel rhythm influxes me into streets, to the petal accent in the warmth tears which is a perfumed life painted in the eyes as solemn as the heat from a proper eloquence of the damned. He sat still and quietly calm, meant to inflict a new kind of kick when the band walked by for the body of your nation and he secretes me the tights of fluxes of an Indian tent where my longing eyes stand to think at the front of a curious brick. There, the heartbeat is solidly given for the up rise of your soul in season. When everything is blindly pure after some thousands of clean lines, our true lure, on and off by remembering a lightning time. The childhood is still delicately divine while a Sempiternal motion in faraway natures could be a brave owner of the free heat. And among some sliding lips of all creatures in the open fidelity as a tender life beat facing with angelical features like fractals. This distant shape runs in our kindness. May this union trade the good couple into the understanding that peace collides with darkness. This early honesty begins as the main classic ruin framed in time with the intent which makes all hymns and for delicate rhymes coming with uncurled matter into the unknown and with personal skies to be felt in visibility as eyes meet skin and they were shown in the departure of your arctic sensibility. May the piano will shed the tears stolen from talent and emerging from a small wonder in this vertigo world where I know you are your own hit sacrament with that heat dream parade being you a giant human. This written way goes with a new bright impulse. Just as if the frozen thick tooth would swear for an uncertain truth in sugar sprayed hearts being seduced for the warm approach as the leaves repose. While sounds flew and rose and the morning uttering stories in us, ascending from a founded glory. Watch the little shy ways always hesitating, looking at spirit's crown as advice and you can draw what you're aiming by turning ashes into some new and thoughtful ice as the melted heart has a dancing melody. Whenever the pillow fights with us along, the night, along the funny way of being strong is alive.

Wanting to offer my sonority in smuggling grace as the jump is still so far away and close to your face. That is me and a dim dime coming closer in the day as you sang about the things that could approach to stay with the movement of braveness that could have your attention. Please, rewind what was your mind as invention; evoke a cosmic smile in every act, your real prolific consequence of being cloud in will. You wonder for that thoughtful feeling walking in your body and you could have taken him to me. I keep you in my own in your birthday meetings as you and I tend to chant a summer and the life of he like a smiling libido into the right warm door of the world. The refrain feeling fine and his proclamation is now dressed in blue with a recreation of this passenger and you are still a little girl. There are calm storms as they are your riding true. The body in kindness has to claim as I face your way of going up there to the taste of a brand-new aim like the candy seeds in an open care given me by a precious conscious in the breaking hour where I focus my love in my lusty eyes around the surface of hermit flour. Is the mirror down from the skies to care and to love, comes the gathering in freedom and you can unite your soul with a bright and cozy wisdom?

When something is on the corner of what is inside the feeling by the verge of knowing the profound scientific sense of the gut in the self-will to ensure what we can do, we should extend the liberation from the rising left wing and right-wing fascism; is like water from a rusty pipe away from a joke, longing for the look inside the same aspect where somewhere deep, we paint the lullaby that makes from the clear floating mirror, a calm chain of desire. The body awakes forever on our first drive around the fresh voice after the sober silence aside the land and with an approach to a frank mood, being blessed by the myriad of books produced by nature and men go in a war. They read then in every tough page of closed meanings. Why? Sometimes the hide and seek is the vestige of the infancy in adults; the silver imagination takes every tree out of honor and with this stolen freedom the political bone of nature's self-will, shall win because it was the first who drove. This is a spontaneous reflection, waiting for repose that my parcel of dreams will work maybe to wonder or predict about the humans with open hearts.

The dream awoke with an outspoken head on the turning idea sooner than should common people undertake as stupid, then what else the dear wisdom can do, rather than feel the tragedy of the gold empire of the State and the Churches being mined with a piece of underwear in this house of love. Yes, dear Manfred, you watched for me in your motor bike where I used to shave at his mirror, we took shower together, yes Lissabon the best city in the world; they robbed all Manfred, I escaped again, it keeps going the taking of my spirit in a forbidden curve where my possessions still satisfy the same humans that are a subjective beauty into the motility of my favorite muse, a fragile woman, delicate and wise to the crowd as these words were made by the sun, dear Patrícia. And the band keeps playing Waltzing Matilda now down in Romania where the milky tricks of the hate the French and German had, is now being taken to the cruelty souvenirs ahead and with the stereo off. May your brother rest in peace and please shut the door, close the curtains, give me again a yogurt I can't stop being inside your room staring at a sea of flashes and your Brian Jones had what were as the tears go by and it is just you on your underwear around this similar fragile figure that cared for the humble black man that I saw today. Close your eyes, this is what I and you had to get it out, of course for me it is clear as I was your existential tutor and you were my muse. Now I am alone in the interval of the same poetical afternoons where the Ocean stands with me, inside the empowering of my poetical body.

Eduardo Alexandre Pinto

Wilhelm Reich and Einstein

Mon May 07, 2012 1:58 am

The only explanation Einstein gave to Reich for not wanting to cooperate with him was that one of Einstein's assistants gave a different explanation of the temperature difference phenomenon. Einstein accepted that different explanation.
The entire Reich-Einstein correspondence is included in Reich's autobiographical book American Odyssey.

For einstein I wanna mention, that einstein didn't take reichs discoveries serious,
in opposite i think he declared them ridiculous and didn't answer for reichs letters
but maybe also that he was blamable touched by reichs info's which made him fear, panic and complexes, which he couldn't stand so he blocked him.

Comment from a liberal friend in Europe

1989

Sun May 06, 2012 3:53 pm

When I was 5 I had my first sexual impulse with a girl at the kindergarten in Lisbon, I refrained myself to play with her because I knew I was going to be punished. At the age of 7 I was forced to go to elementary school against my will, I cried in the first days, then I said to myself that I would chose freedom by intuition of time and it happened. At the school, I introduced sexuality, we the kids were in close touch with our genitals and kissed everywhere at the same time we were oppressed with education. During the 6 years I spent at school I was the best student and athlete. I had respect from all the people of my hometown or most of all, one man, tried to abuse from me at a eletric train, I got rid of him. The historical background of Portugal at that time, was a big sum of social misery while the cowards from the April the 25th of 1974 Portuguese Revolution came back from abroad, they stole more and more as it happened in my family and this is why my parents thought I could help to recover our economy by having an academic degree. At high school I created my freedom, everybody had respect on the heritage of the land, where I belong through my wild temper and since 1986 till 2010, I spent my energy saving lives, more than 100 000 persons, including all kind of animals living in Portugal as well as trees and stones. In 1989, there was a tremendous energy in Lisbon; I met Fakkakboy in that year, seeing him in the spring of 2008 and briefly in the winter of 2009. Many historical things happened in the year of 1989 worldwide.

Expansion is necessary while contraction is the body-mind emotional reaction being an imposed resignation not aware by the masses due to the subtle propaganda through the media and at the streets by the consequent generating social emulation.

In the 21th century I was at close contact with prodigious children both boys and girls but and alike me, we had to survive with money and were forced to abandon our talents by working for the state squad. We are all in close contact, publishing books, painting, sculpting, making music, theatre, ballet, fashion or cinema; culture as hidden paths speaking at the public and all we can do is to spend our time, organizing this chain of lust. Sadly, many young people, died during this process.

Cordially,

Eduardo Alexandre Pinto

Re: The Murder of Christ

Sat Jan 21, 2012 11:34 pm

JFK was the most important politician in the last 60 years. After him no one had his vision of how to embrace past (American Civil War and the carnage over the Indians of the Plains), present and future (OutSpace). Dr. Wilhelm Reich wrote 'The Murder of Christ' predicting what it can happen to good humans...

Fri Oct 28, 2011 12:11 am

JFK was the most important politician in the last 60 years. After him no one had his vision of how to embrace past (American Civil War and the carnage over the Indians of the Plains), present and future (OutSpace). Dr. Wilhelm Reich wrote 'The Murder of Christ' predicting what it can happen to good humans...

Wilhelm Reich

Sat Jan 21, 2012 1:31 pm

When the followers of Alexander Lowen together with the American College of Orgonomy will force the united states government for a public answer in the name of truth and justice, to clean the murderer of Dr. Wilhelm Reich ? America is not a land of freedom, this was Dr. Reich mistake, now only the Wilhelm Reich Museum can defend Dr. Reich legacy and no one else.

Polish the Poetry under Wilhelm Reich teachings

Thu Jan 19, 2012 1:12 pm

If there is a cosmic feeling, I believe so but not the fact that schizophrenia is a mental disorder as others that are labeled in order to make people sleep on their living rooms.

And why Emily Dickinson had freedom on her room for a lifetime or almost? Of course history books refer to her poetry mainly but we cannot separate the sexual harassment on which she was raised and something happened in order to the poetess stayed indoors, writing beautiful and historical poems.

The great designs of hope

Sat Jan 14, 2012 12:55 pm

Human triumph used to suffice and Alexander and I, enemies of this truth, had the pleasure to infer it with a predisposition on the eventual wolf in the breast from a kindled moon's light where the eyes are in care in the seek and believe as an edifying seed of every human need. Fear is now preparing to go away and you will be on my jacket tonight, dear reader, because the sky is open to be watched from one leaf as a bird knows how to hide and seek around the trees with little ways of belonging to the magnitude of a sweet geography like the one who maintains human hope and the honey shape of it as it should be tasted in our table with great content.

Once seen the beauty, once she is well as art of a calm attention where an indigo virtue is a principle of esteem by obtaining her spirit. Love comes along like merit of the origins that compose the zeal in praxis of the double in us and the one among the union is the best harmony within all imperfections. We are the other as flexible example of our perfection by touching and stopping inside the pure repose of beauty. In the plausible awake of life cycles towards the constancy that death is like the fear from the lack of the pure love unity in our lives has the meaning as a continue act of existing. Settling time can and again seed the poetical outcome of the reality of life and death, in short, we can apply the fact that all the radical journalism has its role in the sense that all exists as concern, as feeling and the wrong misrepresentation of life means deaths in many ways of introducing them. You can live with no political bone but you are responsible for a passive voice on the radical acts that mean death and in honor of this escaping, I can only awake and repose on my poetical bones that have the honor in zeal to warn the cycles of existence that a rejuvenation from the psychological deaths can be achieved by sleeping with a virgin or with a child (with no sexual attachment).

We can inspire on the mythological figure of Aesculapius for the settling of a moral rejuvenation in all that concerns pureness in positive standards of bringing information and once taken, we can think, learn, extent her into the origins of life as the great design of hope.

Amoeba

Sun Dec 18, 2011 4:38 pm

Amoeba divides because it cannot tolerate expansion so the genetically issue in here should be understood as a universal law of tension which had derived into the creation of the universe and that the actual conditions of existence are on the same domain as the basis of its creation. Therefore, the reason of the decay of civilizations throughout centuries. What was explained as expansion meant to be a vision of hope with regular care on the liberation of people through sexuality and not by the actual attitude towards the body activity which is a movie career with rational fears led by the carrying of the success of the death instinct. I can only attend prevention while humankind is dressed in the fake moral up against the noble will of the gentle being of the soul. It is not an abandonment of religion but an awake on which many philosophers tried to guide people but not to be commanders of society. They had paid a high price and now all we have is 7 billion whispers.

Children

Mon Nov 21, 2011 1:54 am

I am a writer and I love as the totally of a longing orgasm felt on my house and around the assertive planet of dreams. It is healthy to accept the presence of one hand with voice as the children of the future whisper on their tender lips into the world of warm hopes, it is the cradle of joy and a saying should not be the foundation of the future but the presence of the energy at the hands of the sound of a free recreation because it is poetry and the fun!

Poetry for my first poetical love, Bárbara

Sun Nov 06, 2011 1:28 am

Poetry for my first poetical love, Bárbara: Come in your whistling kind muscles Like that one that by intuition forming a long concentration of Adventure and a baptism of fire when freedom was following my soul arriving at this affair where there is no difference. In songs, the skies, are the spelling moves the crawl of a bell that runs the fist Lampoons on the very cradles that were kissed in the mouth by June is the cherry on the water with the sense of nonprofit? For each cup of feeling I can have a superb read This is seen as what can be felt And so fingers relayed these tunes with me sneaking Aphorisms by the soft twilight Sung as secrets that warm the cold The right-handed and the extreme odor of my heart into heat What a rise into a great breath Signals the grimace that tells you more of this friend In the configuration which blooms in its transformation Knowing that there is life in progress As our body goes into a gentle sleep In a scarlet voice As I am waiting for you, my dream And the strength that can be so much late And here I play as well Tomorrow the heart Of a sacred birth This union of vows and feelings With a localized thinking Living in security Delivers this document because The vein has a whistling breath And the run on the open prairie The foot where your eyes of black honey Smiled once for being too foreign Flanking your look as praise for your skin It's always the time for your encounter In bid to interdict that in your center In every breath and cheered accurate look Among Gordian knots that the same postman Sails, and with the years, the source of values And I would not say that you are here without pain Where we were two per among zillions Above the illustrated and amazed thoughts When the smile is stretching elastic beings The sand here in your arms for the loving And because it's dawn, I estimate to be A mild schism bare-chested A mirror and you're always Home to meet the concise air But as luck of the smooth trot The crease at the neckline courteous November Hip wound me, I'll follow that And the broom makes the holidays that you had A tine thin wide finger It's the greasy touch Connected to the time spent Employed with the attentive soul At sunset, as I recall When looking at this member Suggests that you are undressed And you've got the sky that you dress With that much desire and be late now in praise of my splurge I had signs who sleep and sleeps Read more at whom I weave Passing through years of light Enumerating the name and identity Polishing the voice that seduces me When the rest of happiness Perch in a zillion of steps The Gordian knot gets the green All the uniqueness of your traits Segregating the beat of this seat Your refinement plotting As if was asking What I have in me And so as a nod I tell you that I will be In the hotbed And if I measure what I intuit It's your pout without erasure That the cypress sets As a sensitivity Which runs very thin May be your age That defines what you were born On the horizon you wrote When I was arrested Boiling this heart that is gone Soft sunset I emanate I am like you in the same flames I have for taste, then return In combat as in insurance of thinking Here on Earth in the affairs of heaven Flies with this vision of the veiled And the taste of what makes you dive Being the portion that binds us into two I look you in a manly love pose As having a certain dose with no withdrawals Holding up very well And lifted from your sky Bárbara you are inside a delicate place Revolving around what it might be seen For any life comes without fog And our bed is like love, the first Anointing without blessing somewhere I chimer in the land of nowhere Solemn outdoor And sideways without fainting Who browses cities and nations At the very sly row As the heat of a fire Around the cushion Dozing what I think No pain or census Steadying myself on the horizon In the fascination attached to the bridge A secret tells me that well When I make a hundred The axis and the bond between the royal forces while the route of silence listening to the other corner when I dream, I know by thinking about the landing of our law and a stop parched, stands as a sign if there is also a time of glory light in each cyclical and annual the pace of each life story I give you a handkerchief and a nod because when you think, I will follow you to whistle because of this tension Bent in for your posture, if the thinking plane to land in fertile motions a benign sun for us and the reptile stands quiet at a first touch In young fruit as alive as a trout And we are also against the current And you have the reverse in the handwriting of fire That wrap the tobacco team Which is a metaphor that barricade and seals The benefit of our distraction You came on the side that was our soul And early vines with sweet talk Broke and beautiful as your voice Now in our mouth with love Longing sighs in several years In contrary tones That the tone of this post It's the skin that you see Recent subliminal paintings As your air is heard at the foot of the bed loving bodies in some momentum flows to the resin at the behest which knows how to run and powerfully these maneuvers with sui generous margins Yet this life I feel in distress In the shadows I guess there are splendid truths How to center you Miss?

On the fate of your hip Such a young, frank Radiate as an epic live And in return to know The current extension is either brave As the heat of this generous hand My name drops like a silver star Here on the prairie, where the eye wants to inspect The entanglement of sensuality With dazzling, spinning when geometry in One or two ideas on the space which is aware Patience knows the discerning attention In the mind wanting to travel between arms And the mind appears as a love potion The forearm of dawn Recreating the language of others While the urgency of the hour The echo of your voice at me strolls But the creed of the latent humor What is true for anxiety and amusement Rises by fervor Where is our imprecise ascension I thought your hair as sensitive petal was very appealing to me, invisible and we had this focus altar flowers where you play in this dream too grown The quiet brilliance and Incessant ecstasy Embrace the look of this wave Giving you my daughter My infant dream For your heart can walk And I'm in physical time Wanting to calm your smile my dear On a nice cloud for you in praise By the softness of this love.

Ed

Healing through sounds

Wed Nov 02, 2011 4:18 pm

Águas is one handicapped woman on which I awake her libido through sounds and she could feel pleasure for the first time on her life with the age of 35.

Love, Prejudice and Economy

Wed Nov 02, 2011 3:43 pm

I could observe a shame over masturbation on the European youth and a similar decay in all generations regarding sexuality because people prefer the immediate pleasure rather than to feel and talk as friends do. The love problem is an emotional one and this is our reality. I am aware that the pure love is not to stand due to economy.

The Sempiternal Pansexuality

Sat Oct 29, 2011 3:29 am

Affection is a candy nerve that needs to be caressed like a nipple in the heart of contentment.
One thought with wide distance to the words of any life commencement is a spasmodic teardrop and everybody wants to find the same approach who defines the landscape where sunshine is painted in the best portrait of the perpetual finitude while there is an appealing sky to attend in the love act between the reading of nature and the rise of beauty in clean white souls.
Nothing remains forever and you can come to this event with cherries and a red towel to stand in the grass for a pick-nick where the darkness turns blue as I see you running
to the sunny days of the world´s infancy.
We were born as we felt in the first feeling of silence to be here and appearing
to cry our steamy energy. The frequency of irradiating moods is heard on the laughing lines of the character, either in love or in hate. Hate delivers emotions to the heart of destruction with all it was said and done in order to unite the irrational with the unique aggressions thrown in the social environment like crimes and stories of the possessed in the living theatre of absurd but if lucidity comes at the time of acting as instinct of peace, then feelings will be tender like the long fidelity of silence.

Biological Wisdom

Thu Oct 27, 2011 3:00 pm

Inside a tear whereas the topography of a character is built up with the movements of our shoulders as a part of the love vision that stands at a distance from the dawn into the epic light of being inside the repose of a leaf and the wise song lies also inside this logic because it breathes like a selected poem from the estuaries and shores as part of an ancient attraction into all epic thoughts that had turned real, a leaf knows why. Humans pitch the babies from the ideal environment like the rain forest; no revolution can be other than a sexual revolution, we must dive on the white hope of existence in order to understand the satisfaction of this movement. Economy is powder, in exact or close exchange the lifeblood turns the pink heart of one funny cartoon into the electric add of a mutual intercourse, mainly because we are as seasons, we dive to seek the closest nest around our biological wisdom as humans from a funny planet.

The Biological Verses of Wisdom

Thu Sep 29, 2011 12:57 pm

Copyright from LAP Lambert Academic Publishing, 2011

The Biological Verses of Wisdom

People prefer to live according to games without frontiers rather than to accept truth. I could observe it for a long period of time with professional bandits being in or out of the governments list. In fact, there is a list organized by the same people which ask me for support.
It is something sick and sad.
The world is filled with extreme severity, to change this reality takes many of the superimpositions on which people are devoted and this irrationality leads the same world of people into a misrepresentation of the social intercourse, then the wars, some small, some huge, tough the events are real as the misery in human relations. Envy is accepted and adored, the examples are too many, look at the top of everything related to consume even in books and you will understand why society tends to put people indoors.
One musician David Byrne said that Poetry was on the streets, it is easy because he never skins himself alive to save people from the actual state of societies and their behavior. My role is to explain at the same time that I must save myself from this sick fever that my naked intuition that acts worldly like a boomerang. I can feel it.
To calculate and to organize the things as manners of many decals of a

certain anxiety which lead me to think about the rush of the necessary changes as chances to obtain a release so similar into what Jews went through. Is difficult to attend beauty in this way, I can recall my former relations and drink from their best while the late-night bath was a way to induce me into more thinking. It is thinking that commands my life. It is one friendly command as it seduces the work of many people´s anxieties and in this way, I can understand on how and by a proper method I can regain the calm which had went into the body as engine of reason. Once I wrote about instinct and reason and I can related them into the facts that my father went through in Mozambique when he could not see the enemy. If the talking is right then the results are also good. Meaning the understanding of the ego nudity in the realm of its movement and by the activity on the conscious rational and on the sub conscious level; the equilibrium on the deepest form when men and women are deep, honest, gentle is the gain for the future. To understand the anger on each of us despite the civilization threads is important.

What I had learned from this day, was that all the former notes had a reason to be written and I also understood how Subtleties can be endorsed as the role of an author.

Sexuality is far as the love as well while the fascists occupy their seats and the people clap like bozos with no plankton because it is gone, I can collect my health, the wolf eyes up on every mountain and leaving another dream for tomorrow.

I have prosthesis but I don´t use her because in this way no girl will like me though I seek and believe that there must be a woman on which I can love on its full length and I will seek till the end of my existence and not like a character of a movie but as a real person.

I used to smoke one cigarette every week at my high school, I felt great, I was seated at one rectangular stone, the perception of the world was pure, and maybe someone had felt her, since I had one nymph from one street that surrounds the lyceum as one unknown figure from the same street friend of a fake friend called Alexandra Parrado that like Carlos Parreira, both were never in touch with my realm with continuity.

Loyalty seems to be erased in the name of the immediate fucks and economy.

I am feeling good things from the world, small but huge as living examples of moral beauty.

While the mean tries to attack each day, resistance holds with a reckless determination, justice will be done with the necessary courage and resistance against the Ming and the Yo-Yo people, always up and down especially when you're happy to show your joie de vivre; at this stage, they want everything and the opposite they disregard with great cruelty as beasts they are.

I wonder why the book, ´Fury on Earth´ by Myron Sharaf is out of the archives of http://www.archive.org.

San Tiago cliff is one of the most inspiring places on which I have been and felt, with people and alone. There was a road from there into Escurquela, once I and my father crossed this road on a green Mercedes with a goat on the backseat. It was a hot day.

Sometimes I have to be cautious like San Tiago and take a rest from all the flying Dutchmen and the swindlers of the station where the station stopped like in Viseu, a land of fascists.

My tribute to Mr. Curt Bois a refined gentleman who taught into Cassiel what is the role of the narrator of humankind, so solemn and humble. I remember how a senior got rid of 3 skinheads inside a train. I personally change from carriage to carriage by instinct.

Also14 years ago, I could point my penis into the driver head toward the future on the way to Sintra. I made a thunder operation in the year of 1991 or 1992 into Queluz.

Eliza was the lover of my Grand-Father, she had worked for Mr. Orlando Ferreira and his wife Mrs Maria Teresa and she has been so bad treated by his relatives at Rua General Taborda, number 15, second floor. I know her house, she a kind woman. The Dalmatian called Egas which I used to walk with Raquel died.

Raquel is one distant cousin that I had love. We used to play in full joy. I miss her.

The last time I saw her, she was in her room. She has delicate eyes and manners, elegant and beautiful.

For years I thought of her. There were more children on which we all played together in happiness. Marco fell in the tank of my Great-Uncle Miguel. Uncle Miguel was a beautiful man, he used to lie down on a long chair to relax and him and his wife, Mrs. Cassilda used to drive a blue Volkswagen into the Vila Real and everybody in Lugar da Coutada, especially the kids, my friends, were happy. Everybody looked with astonished to their departure. Magic times, of course the danger was immanent and the pigs came to stay. Once he pointed at us a riffle because we the kids were eating the Golden kind of so many apples in his lands that were from my Grand Father. He felt bad once, he told to Mr. Avelino, our neighbor, the father of Marco and Cristina (his wife is called Emília, a kind and good cooker, I have good memories of them, despite what had happened later with the European money; but the fact is that he died and Cassilda stayed alone sewing with the women from Coutada. In 1994, my Grand- Mother died. I remember the yellow car from their relatives. At the funeral of my Grand-Mother my aunt could not stand and stayed at Pedregal. Zé Duarte blessed, my cousin Amândio (which abused from me, to have land for cheap price to build a house), at the same time, my cousin Fausto died after scorning at me in a good way. The father of Zé Duarte was known as Couratas, he had a gun as well as Mr. Frias. My father had a Mouser, so I was told by him. Probably yes and he should and so should I.

I brought my room from Tapados into Santo António da Caparica.

There must be a living person in the world which whom I can make close contact. I am in love with a woman which has 200 years and having a good friend being a science man which died in 1957.

I guess I still can hold the dawn like I did between 1991 and 1994 in here.

Cristina Ventura Arias, wrote me as dedication of ´The Myth of Sisyphus´ by Albert Camus, the following:

Sísifo estaba condenado a subir una montaña con una gran pedra, durante toda la eternidad. Es un mito, pero como todo mito tiene una parte de verdad a la que el hombre está condenado a combatir. Hay que combatir las coordenadas de Sísifo y hay que dejar de esperar a Godot. Te dedico este libro, por seres buen guerrero.

Muchos besos de tu amiga Cristina.

Madrid, Junio 2010.

Once Alexander met Carlos Paião at the subway station of Roma in Lisbon, later he died in a car accident on the way to the North.

Alexander was completely alone since around 1:30 am from Galicia till 4:45 am, in the

heart of the Galician mountains where he could take care of big horses as good

friends in the year of 1997, April. When he arrived at a small village a good woman served him a coffee, he ate chocolate and smoked Spanish cigarettes. He saw on TV, Saramago, in June both met at Parque Eduardo VII.

Alex saw a girl at Marquês de Pombal, she was brave kind, they looked at each other.

I remember the prostitute which said that my penis was pretty. I had many prostitute friends, one used to salute me when I was 12 on the way to my high school. She was kind.

Later I met one that took me into Casal Ventoso which I knew from the frequent visits of Miguel Ângelo, with him I was not scared, later I went with Sara a bisexual girlfriend from Leiria.

I guess I belong into the world. What can I do has gotten me big, black, yellow, green as blue too.

Chapter VIII

A Growing Saying Before the Fall

I could prove today into myself after about 17 hours that my poetical condition is well. Somehow, I am conspicuous since the beginning.

The danger on today's societies is not only the full extension of control, I will lead this thought open into the reader.

My mother used to call me, ´o miúdo da bica´.

I have never had a hometown. I was doing things like doing love like a fool, I guess I am inside new and old times as a glorified feature on my soul and probably I had recaptured my personal youth through consistent work all around and always inside as far as I can be.

Daniel, a German boy was using a hatchet, I was in stress, suddenly my aunt Leonor called on the edge of a racking feeling. We ate together, smoked together, then another German boy which drove told me about him and aside me on the backseat, two young German boys were caressing their fingers with their guitars. I was looking to the landscape, I could see the sea. I am made of many rivers, once I got a phone call from the Nile.

Alexander, I am wondering about eternity as if writing would be the right way.

In June of 2008 at the front of Station de Francia in Barcelona, one woman in a motorbike had an accident, the paramedics appeared in less than 5 minutes. She was bleeding, I watched the medical procedures and then went for a walk where I found a web coffee, I met there one American cheater and one Australian cheater, both women.

Again, the same existential exhaustion, it comes and goes like the will into sexuality.

Last night I fell asleep naked, some people had block me from masturbation.

It is almost sunset, I saw them in so many places like they would be felt like my post box in Tapados de Baixo where I have received one postcard from Ana Cristina.

So many things happened since I met Bárbara, I see myself writing under the April Skies, under the April sun. Sometimes it rains when I am furious. The thunders in Escurquela that my father felt. He used to bath on the tank, I saw him once naked.

Alexander used to wash himself near the fountain. All the interval of time from the events that took place were the irrational behavior of social envy and social fear, either by individuals either by organized. Wilhelm Reich was right, he did not fear to go ahead despite of Freud´s sense of guilt and fear. I felt fear because I am involved in so many things and they come like a boomerang and the vice versa effect.

A judge and a psychiatrist were the last beautiful women on whom I had to face, I wonder what they are doing now. Wish to find my personal sand.

Alexander likes risk, only this way he can feel the adrenaline inherent to his nature. He used to go far to play football at every place, he played for 22 years in all positions. His favorite shirt had a question mark in green. His favorite chemise is grey, this chemise follows his adventures for more than 15 years. He needs a bonnet now.

Dona Maria Helena, known to be the wife of the Judge liked cats, she challenged the owner of a garage bravely. She died at the phone. We were friends. She was similar to Ingrid Bergman.

Seldom my infinite intelligence provides me many questions like the Leipzig emptiness where a Chinese female voice was inside me.

Sometimes I wake myself and awake the gain of living as my generous Sempiternal feelings.

Today for example, 23 years later and again I proved into my philosophy teacher that I was right on the second discussion between both and that was about the hermit situation; a hermit can cure himself.

I think that the sea smiles.

Museums do smile they are the rejuvenation of time as virgins and children are.

I guess I have to seek like I used to do with Isabel.

I am emotional with my memories which are real, this is no movie. All my life I had fought and when I think about my Polish teacher, I feel touched. I was and I am at the bottom of existence like being inside a woman, deeply at the most hidden sensibility of the uterus. An endless rain came to pitch the sayings of my soul as if Isabel Allende would be here.

I could understand the danger from the differences that exist between me and the crowd.

It took me a cold temper to solve a small dilemma that has the meaning to enhance and to diminish my strengths. The necessary comprehension of my personality in order to understand this difference lies on my soul. You have to enter on me with in calm and the world around will be also calm.

Tarzan Taborda lived in Fonte da Telha, he was a wrestler known to fought for a long period of time and the story tells that he could place 160 000 persons at one stadium in Saudi Arabia. Later while he was getting old, he had challenged one young karate fighter and the former gave up on the duet.

I saw a small lizard and a red sportive Opel, I like both. My bible has the image of many white vehicles in Jerusalem. Luis Filipe Sebastião has the rare edition of Baudelaire´s book, ´Les Fleurs du Mal´ which I stole from my favorite library.

I remember the hands of João Fonseca on the way of so many people´s lyceum, Maria Amália Vaz de Carvalho.

A person with a certified idea on his mind let´s say, it has the ethic right to present him into the world but he cannot by any other way, to impose it into the others.

Sometimes and I speak from what I feel, the invisible emotional ties can block the good advance of the mind in action and her ideas. There are and it is visible the attacks from the people which cannot fully understand the gender of truth in regard as it matters this free discipline.

Guterres once went into Belém do Pará and for who doesn´t know, there it rains every day at the same time, the people who were looking at him; they all went away when the rain had come. Every year I have my especial soap from there. They are packed in illustrated paper with a certain sensibility when you open it and later you bath yourself with them. I remember the smell of Susana Cunha and from Margarita a little. I had the idea in 1997 to go into Paris and take a sample of my semen because it was so perfumed.

I met Lígia Soares in the first weekend of September of that year.

One Husky was nervous because the dog was shy before he held a sled race and the owner could calm him.

I phoned a friend and a similar feeling came like when I was listening Mozart. I found someone to talk too while I don´t know someone that lies on my interests, her name is above the air. I could hear the voice of Pan Pawel Dambek, he used to make a gesture on the neck which I thought it meant to shave but it meant to drink.

I had to write for the President of the United States because the actual situation is extremely unfair and I add a few thoughts on my message, hoping that Mr. Obama will think of the mess Americans are doing it for

200 hundred years. It was a tough day,
I had to bring a saying of more than 30 years into my mind while I was fighting the local atrocities and even crying from so much lack of education around me since some years.

Alexander could be quiet while these events were present. So the passing present must learn with the past in an organized way, in order to preserve the future while we are able to think.

To understand the boiling waters on the sand you and they have to claim your own way to feel as what it can stand to enter the peace command.

I was with great delight with children in a train and we had fun all together. I don't need to be in an organized place to play with children. I think they are sleeping now.

Dr. Wilhelm Reich could and saying it again, the vision of the income of energy on which Emily Dickinson and I were and are involved, making from the splendor of our poetry, being indoors or from outdoors, pieces of extreme beauty. I feel the poetry in my fur closely similar in care with Emily's fur. So, who will come after the two of us?

That is the question on which I am involved while I write my thoughts.

Alexander thinks of Jesus and why were both with prostitutes. Like Phil Collins would say, I don't have all the answers, though I think that we had found a great deception and had to kick the richness from all mother tongues with great irritation. While Buddha was sleeping all the time; so, the question is: Do people with vision can have a life with dignity?

It seems difficult that after 200 centuries nothing has changed on this matter. I can only complain and to preach in my poetical silence as a personal heat paraded in one place or in many places as art of living.

People don't devote much time to their interior and after billions of deaths leading as examples to the world into nothing concrete than emptiness, I feel the same and Emily was wiser because she kept the quietness.

Moses was 40 years in the desert, the bible states that he lived 800 hundred years and I think it was possible because his people didn't need to throw things into the land but to walk upon the land until those people could see the light. Natural laws of existence have their characteristics and if people on today's societies can at least understand to be caressed by this gentle shadow, then it is so much easier to hold and to handle all the things that can be admired as self-satisfaction.

Alexander had the will to find a dark brown woman with a brave spirit and a young boy which could by his own characteristics seek his legacy as a human. Alexander knows that he has the soul in the character as the defender of the world.

I found in an image made by thoughts the mental exercise that was the contemplation condition. I don't know which energy led me into the Soito cliff but I went it in calm and had achieved calm. Till the compact bodies of hard people had come to destroy the magnificence of this spontaneous beauty.

Some people had released all the dogs but I was sorry to make them sad, I really am not afraid of dogs.

About the saying well is hidden under the title above this chapter, you have to find him.

I know that my backyard is unseen by the love which I have since ever and where no man or woman had felt what I had from there, neither wherever I was, since my muscles are as agile as my thoughts.

Everyone can teach something.

Now the bandits arrived into Santo António da Caparica, it is 4:41 a.m. they had come drunk as they think alcohol is food.

I hate them.

In fact, the world is heading into a massive destruction and there is nothing I can do about it.

Hours after I awoke, in the interval of this I could hear a woman screaming with her sexual feelings and she inspired me to forgive into the world at least for the necessary time for them to think about the mess it exists. They had scorn from many people who tried to make social changes, so the time is of great attention and care for the things that my eyes attend on this matter.

Isabel came to attend Alex's thoughts while existence was handling with their daily things, some things were on his mind as the Soito cliff feeling. There is one truth and that is reality, on my case is a poetical reality taken as a natural love sadly not understood.